P9-DMF-093

Sins and Needles

Sins and Needles

A Story of Spiritual Mending

Ray Materson

and

Melanie Materson

Algonquin Books of Chapel Hill 2002

Published by
ALGONQUIN BOOKS OF CHAPEL HILL
Post Office Box 2225
Chapel Hill, North Carolina 27515-2225

a division of Workman Publishing
708 Broadway
New York, New York 10003

Printed in China.
Published simultaneously in Canada by Thomas Allen & Son Limited.
Design by Janet Vicario.

Library of Congress Cataloging-in-Publication Data
Materson, Ray, 1954–
Sins and needles : a story of spiritual mending / Ray Materson and Melanie Materson.
p. cm.
ISBN 1-56512-340-9
1. Materson, Ray, 1954– 2. Needleworkers—United States—Biography. 3. Narcotic addicts—United States—Biography. 4. Prisoners as artists—United States. I. Materson, Melanie, 1958– II. Title.
NK9298.M38 A2 2002
365'.6'092—dc21
[B] 2002018670

10 9 8 7 6 5 4 3 2 1
First Edition

All events in this book are true. Names have been changed to protect the privacy of some individuals.

To our children

Acknowledgments

We wish to thank Aarne Anton of American Primitive Gallery for his many years of encouragement, friendship, and work; Victoria Wilson for her belief in this book and for introducing us to our brilliant and hardworking agent Martha Kaplan; Tom Patterson for his knowledge, support of this project, and initial editing work; Elisabeth Scharlatt, Andra Olenik, and all the people at Algonquin Books; Ann Gati for her friendship and help in the early days; Sam Connor and Jeffrey Green for their work with prison artists; Harrison "Whitey" Jenkins; Thomas Lail and Tara Fracalossi; Steve Nalepa, Jodi Wiley, and Nick Rubenstein; Ann Savageau and Joshua Moyer for completeing the circle for Ray at University of Michigan; Dan Slivatz for his friendship that has withstood the test of time; Rebecca Hoffberger and everyone at the American Visionary Art Museum; the congregations at Avery Street Christian Reformed Church, South Windsor, Connecticut, and First Church (Reformed) in Albany, New York; Pastors Doug Vanderwall, Berton VanAntwerpen, Pacia Vamvas, LeRoy Suess, and Gregg Mast for their spiritual guidance and emotional support; and the staff and administration at the CT Correctional Institutions (Somers and Enfield) who encouraged Ray's artistic endeavors. We also wish to thank the many media writers and reporters who have shared the optimism and hope of this story with the many readers who seek it; and all the collectors of Ray's artwork, especially WLD. Finally, a special thank-you to Irene Materson and Barbara Burk.

1. The House on York Road

The big, east-facing front porch was trellised on its southern side. In the summer, small pink roses reached out in all directions, from the lush, black earth to the eave of the roof. Grandma Hattie would regularly sit in a rocking chair in the shade of the trellis and work her embroidery. A compact woman with a hunched back and a nose like a hawk's beak, she had spent most of her life in Brooklyn, but she'd come to live with us after the death of my uncle Eddie, who had always looked after her. She was almost eighty at the time, and Dad insisted that she move in with us. It was an arrangement that caused my mother a good deal of apprehension, and it seemed that my grandmother was less than delighted with the social and geographic change. But Dad was a man who felt deep familial obligation, so Grandma Hattie—with her housecoats, gaudy jewelry, dentures, sewing basket, and out-of-place Brooklyn accent—had become a member of the family.

I was eight years old when we moved into the large, four-bedroom house on the corner of York Road and Meadowbrook Drive in Parma Heights, Ohio. It was the summer of 1962, and we'd left Grand Rapids, Michigan, because my father had taken a transfer from his employer, an insurance company. Our new house was beautiful, with rich woodwork and beveled-glass windows. On sunny days these windows projected slow-moving rainbows across the floors and walls. Dad, Mom, Grandma Hattie, my sister, Barbara, and I enjoyed a shared fantasy that there were little pots of gold at the end of each rainbow.

It took a little time for me to fully adjust to the move to Parma Heights, but I fell in love with the expansive backyard and the pear trees out front—and I enjoyed meeting the other kids who lived in the neighborhood. It was during my four and a half years on York Road that I learned to play baseball, developed an appreciation for the theater, and earned a measure of popularity among my peers.

My best friend was Mike Sforzo, who lived two doors up the road from us. His older sister, Darlene, was a high-school classmate of my sister's at Nazareth Academy, a Catholic girls school, and that's how I'd come to know him. A year older than I, Mike excelled at sports: baseball, football, and boccie. I never matched his athletic abilities, but that never lessened my love of sports, especially baseball.

In the suburbs of Cleveland, most of the other neighborhood kids claimed the Indians as their favorite team. But I delighted in rooting for the New York Yankees. They were the team to be reckoned with, and their star players—Mickey

Mantle, Whitey Ford, Bobby Richardson, and Roger Maris—were my heroes. I read about them in the *Plain Dealer,* listened to their games on a rocket-shaped red, crystal-receiver radio, and watched their televised games against the Indians with intense concentration. Once, when I was about ten years old, my sister won tickets to a Yankees-Indians game in an academic competition. Our whole family (except Grandma Hattie) attended the game at Cleveland's Municipal Stadium. At one point in the game—which the Yankees won—the Mick came within ten or twelve rows of our seats when he ran to catch a foul ball that was dropping near the stands. I felt sure he'd seen me.

Perhaps it was the naïveté of childhood, or maybe it had something to do with being raised as a Roman Catholic, but a sense of security enveloped me during my childhood. I knew I had a guardian angel always looking over my shoulder, as the nuns at Holy Family School had assured me. When it came to truth, God was the only higher authority than the priests and nuns at Holy Family.

I started school there in the third grade. The class was large and well disciplined. Boys wore gray slacks, white shirts, and string ties that were clasped at the neck with a Holy Family medallion. Girls wore gray plaid jumpers, white blouses, knee socks, and saddle shoes. If we wanted to stand out, we knew it had to be for our actions. The uniforms contributed to the general sense of order and discipline.

School started each morning with Mass. We would meet in our classrooms, and after the roll was called, we'd walk single file, girls followed by boys, to the church on the opposite side of the parking lot and playground. Talking or straying out of line was strictly forbidden, because—as Father Benechek often said—God created an orderly universe, and he expects nothing less from his children, the crown of his creation.

Holy Family Church was a big, unostentatious, red-brick structure attached to the school's gymnasium and auditorium. The interior was modestly ornate, with statues of Saint Joseph and the Blessed Virgin, as well as the Holy Family. Each of us was expected to remain silent while considering our uniqueness, our sinful nature, and the saving grace of Christ the Redeemer. I loved all of it, and I envied the older boys who were fortunate enough to be selected to serve on the altar alongside the priest. But I was painfully aware that I couldn't begin training as an altar boy until I was in the sixth grade. Or so I thought.

In November of my third-grade year, I was selected to play the role of a traveling priest in a Christmas play. The story line involved a pioneer family stranded in their log cabin during a snowstorm, unable to attend the traditional midnight Mass on Christmas Eve. My character—lost, hungry, and suffering from frostbite and exposure—stumbled upon the cabin by fortunate accident and was nursed back to health just in time to hold the midnight Eucharist celebration. I believed Sister Mary

Theresa when she told us it was a true story about answered prayers.

Thus it was that I celebrated my first Mass at the age of eight—and as a priest, no less! The experience was so rich and spiritually invigorating that I couldn't let go of it. So, in the priestly vestments that my mother had sewn for me out of old satin curtains, I began frequently celebrating Mass at home in my bedroom. I flattened and shaped pieces of white bread to form my make-believe Eucharist hosts. And, with the meticulous assistance of my sister—who would've been proud to have her brother become a priest someday—I constructed all the mandatory accoutrements, from the altar to candlesticks and a chalice. I conducted the services for a hand-me-down teddy bear and a stuffed panda—neither of whom accepted Communion.

2. Humiliated

My young life was not without its humiliations. After a stunning third-grade year and a summer that saw the Yankees once again contending for the pennant, I looked forward to beginning the fourth grade. I'd been warned, though, that my teacher was to be the much feared Sister Judith, famous for whacking the backs of her students' hands with a metal-edged ruler for the slightest infraction. Still, with my stellar academic record and my guardian angel at my side, I was confident that I'd become Sister Judith's favorite pupil in no time.

Students arrived early for the first day of class at Holy Family School, and the sunny weather on that September day allowed us to gather on the parking lot and playground. Most of us arrived on foot from the surrounding neighborhoods. I looked for familiar faces I hadn't seen during the summer and talked with neighborhood friends about baseball cards. Over the summer I'd managed to collect the entire starting lineup for the Yankees. I turned down an offer from Mark Becker to pitch cards. I knew I'd risk losing valuable cards in such a gambling exchange, not to mention the danger of getting the corners of my cards crimped.

There were two fourth-grade classes, each composed of thirty to forty students. After the roll was taken we were led into the school. Sister Judith's classroom was on the main floor of the sprawling, old brick building, just past a statue of a kindly-looking Saint Joseph. Many of us made the sign of the cross as we passed the statue, in reverence to the saint himself as well as in petition to the Almighty that our knuckles would be spared Sister Judith's wrath.

The classroom was large, and the wall opposite the door was lined with windows that overlooked the parking lot and playground. Another wall was lined with shelves of readers, color-coded according to ability level, along with a variety of other books, each stamped with a nihil obstat and imprimatur, indicating that an ecclesiastical council had designated them as approved reading material. Desks were arranged in six perfect rows of five, six, or seven, and in a corner at the front of the room was an American flag. Nearby, a large crucifix loomed over Sister Judith's gray metal desk, which was stacked with books and study guides. The blackboard was spotless, and the chalk tray underneath it contained not a speck of dust—just an uncommonly thick-looking yardstick.

We filed into the classroom and selected our desks, the girls taking the three rows nearest the window. Many of the lift-top desks were new, with a Formica surface. I chose an older-looking wooden-topped desk, about three seats from the front of the class and next to a row of girls. After sitting down, I noticed a grave imperfection: Carved into the upper-right-hand corner of the desktop and highlighted with blue ink was CCDA 1492. My initial reaction bordered on shock. I'd never seen a piece of school property defaced. We'd been repeatedly told that marking up desks or other school property was tantamount to defacing the Cross of Jesus. It was unthinkable! But I had already stowed my binder, notebooks, pencils, and pen inside the storage compartment. The class session was about to begin, and there were no other desks available. I was trapped in the sinful and imperfect one, overcome with a feeling of dread.

Sister Judith stood at the front of the room, called for silence, and said a prayer to bless our class and our studies. After calling out our names in alphabetical order, she asked us to open our desktops so that she could see if everyone had the proper supplies. A tall, severe-looking woman, Sister Judith had a high-bridged nose, a wide, thin-lipped mouth, and thick, dark eyebrows that stood out prominently against the crisp white covering of her wimple. She totally commanded the classroom space as she walked, like an inspector general, up and down the aisles of desks.

She moved through the classroom, stopping at each desk

to look at the contents. Occasionally she would ask about a missing item. As I waited for Sister's inspection of my supplies, I considered the inscription carved into the top of my desk. Suddenly it occurred to me: CCDA 1492 was a reference to Christopher Columbus and his discovery of America! It was an academic reference! And I had figured it out. As Sister Judith approached my desk, a quiet pride came over me. I was even hoping she would ask me about it.

After Sister Judith checked my supplies, she looked down at my desk.

"And what, Master Materson, does CCDA 1492 mean?"

Feeling sure that I would really impress Sister, I respectfully responded, "Sister, that stands for Christopher Columbus discovered America in 1492!"

"And did you carve that into your desk, Master Materson?" she demanded.

"Why, no, Sister Judith," I stammered, caught completely off guard by the suggestion.

She took a half step toward me. "Well, I think you did. You defaced school property, and I think you're lying as well."

I had nothing to offer in my defense. I was embarrassed and ashamed to the point of tears. To emphasize her disgust, the puffy, round-faced girl who sat next to me glared and muttered, "Tsk, tsk, tsk." The same wordless exclamation made its way around the girls' side of the room. The other boys averted their eyes when I looked to them for some kind of quiet support. I felt like I had tarnished the Cross of Jesus. I wanted to become invisible.

In the days and weeks that followed, nothing more was said about the desktop. I did all that I was supposed to do as a student in Sister Judith's class. Yet I lived under the shadow of fear that the topic might come up again. Even though it didn't, and I quietly finished the year with straight A's, some residue of the shame I had felt on that first morning lingered on.

But then, humiliation was a feeling I had already learned to live with, thanks to my father.

3. An Impossible Man

His life was gentle, and the elements
So mixed in him that Nature might stand up
And say to all the world, "This was a man!"

My sister quoted those lines from Act V of *Julius Caesar* more than twenty years ago, when she eulogized our father. He had often quoted Shakespeare to us, as he had Plato, Aristotle, Spinoza, Thoreau, and the Bible. An amateur philosopher, painter, and poet, Dad was fond of intellectual meandering and expounding on subjects ranging from the nature of the cosmos to the ways in which the meaning of life is played out in sixty minutes of gridiron action on Sunday-afternoon television during the fall. Our father: a mixture of the elements.

His life, however, was anything but gentle. He had seen the ravages of war during the Normandy invasion, the deaths of three older brothers, and the misdiagnosis and subsequent lifelong institutionalization of a fourth brother. He loathed conformity and trusted almost no one. He hated the insurance industry, which paid our bills, and he often reviled it as a business that produced nothing but paperwork and false security.

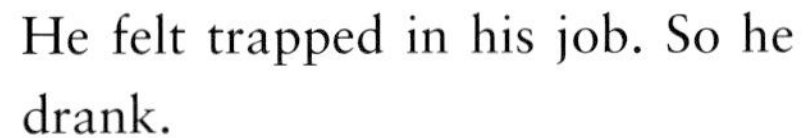

He felt trapped in his job. So he drank.

He drank almost daily, and always to excess. I remember hiding from him as he raved and shouted and called everyone in our family cruel names. Because he valued intelligence, Barbara and I worked hard to maintain the highest possible grades at school. Yet to come home showing off an A paper or class report often meant having it torn up in front of my face and listening to a lengthy treatise on the subject of humility as a virtue. It was rare indeed for anyone to manage to please him. We hated him, but we also loved him and couldn't imagine life without him.

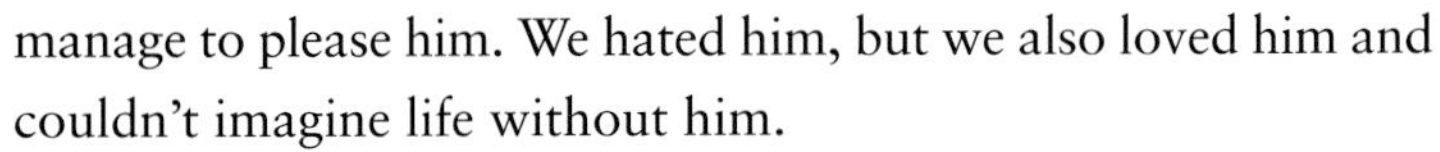

Long before he died, when Barbara and I were still children, we had an opportunity to find out what it was like to live without him for a while. It was in 1965, during my sixth-grade year at Holy Family School. The Vietnam War was in its early stages of escalation, and for Dad it was a source of tremendous anger, sadness, and antigovernment feelings. Every night, as he watched the NBC evening news, he would cry in obvious agony as the latest footage from the war zone was shown, as if the dead and wounded soldiers were his own lost brothers. Then he would explode with litanies of profanity directed at the politicians who were regularly shown issuing dire warnings about the necessity of stopping the Communist menace.

"It's these sons of bitches who are the menace!" he would shout, his eyes bulging and a snakelike vein popping out on his forehead as he pointed a trembling forefinger at the glowing screen in our living room.

The rest of our family came to hate the nightly news, because in Dad it triggered uncontrollable, alcohol-fueled rages that inevitably continued well into the prime-time TV hours and sometimes into the early mornings. Once anchormen Chet Huntley and David Brinkley said their good-nights, we knew we were in for another night of hell. Dad would redirect his explosive anger toward us, as though we were to blame for the carnage in Southeast Asia. Grandma Hattie was usually in bed by that time, asleep behind her locked door, so she was spared his wrath. As for the rest of us, we learned to flee and hide. Sometimes we'd go to the attic, sometimes to the workshop in the cellar. When things got really out of hand, we'd leave the house and sleep in the car, often until daybreak. We'd take turns running reconnaissance missions to the back door to listen for signs that he was still awake. We made jokes about it, pretending we were the good guys in a cowboy movie, checking to see that the coast was clear. We laughed and cried and held on to each other for dear life.

Mom constantly apologized to us for marrying Dad in the first place. She had met him when she was a sales clerk for Eastman Kodak in New York City, where she grew up. He was a handsome young man mutual friends had introduced to her shortly before World War II ended.

"He wasn't like this when I married him!" she would exclaim, sobbing, as we took refuge from Dad's tirades.

Dad's ravings about the war continued for many months, until—finally, during a shouting match with him—Mom yelled back, "If you're so concerned about what's happening in Vietnam, then why don't you go there and do something about it! Why don't you just go there already!"

Within two months, he was gone, commissioned as a junior engineer aboard a U.S. Merchant Marine vessel, on his way to Southeast Asia.

4. **HERO IN ABSENTIA**

My year in sixth grade was an eventful one. I was on the school track team, and I was elected class president. I wrote, directed, produced, and starred in two school plays, one about dental hygiene and the other based on the *Mr. Ed* television sitcom series, about a talking horse. Also during that year, I developed my first crush—on a freckle-faced girl named Jolene. She had been my main competition for the class presidency, and we also competed for top academic honors. I walked her home from school and carried her books. I longed for something more in the relationship, but I never mustered the nerve to kiss her. So we remained rivals and the best of friends.

At home we missed Dad, despite our all-too-vivid memories of what he was like to live with, and when his occasional letters arrived, with postage stamps from places we were hearing about on the news, we scrambled to read them. They contained little mention of the war and were mostly filled with assurances that he looked forward to returning home. One thing was certain: It was much quieter around our house, a relief to all of us.

Dad's presence in Southeast Asia did give me a new sense of pride in him. I imagined him attacking enemy machine-gun nests and single-handedly saving the lives of his fellow marines. He was actually in the merchant marines, but when I mentioned him to my friends, I chose to drop the word *merchant,* because it didn't fit my John Wayne images of war and brave men taking death-defying risks. Thus did Dad become in absentia a hero to me. Every day as I looked at the photograph of him in his marine uniform—prominently displayed in my bedroom—I felt that I loved him more than ever. But I was glad he was halfway around the world.

Sometime in the spring of 1966, less than a year after Dad's departure, we received an airmailed letter from the Philippines announcing that he was coming home. At first we were elated. I imagined air force jets flying overhead, twenty-one-gun salutes, and parades of soldiers marching to John Philip Sousa tunes. But as the news sank in, the only sound you might have heard was the painfully soft thud our hearts made as they dropped in unison there on York Road.

Mom tried to assure all of us—herself included—that things would be different this time. "This is something your dad needed to do," she explained. "He'll feel better about himself now." Her optimism was infectious, overriding any doubts that Barbara and I had, so we hoisted banners of hope in our hearts and planned for the safe return of our father.

Then, one evening in May, we all climbed into our red 1963 Plymouth Valiant for the two-hour drive to Toledo and the merchant port on Lake Erie. Grandma Hattie dressed up for the occasion in her biggest, gaudiest jewelry and a turbanlike hat. Barbara's comments about the turban were met with scolding responses from our grandmother, who believed that a woman needed to wear a hat in order to be properly dressed for a special occasion. That topic consumed us for most of the trip, diverting our attention from our unspoken fears.

My first glimpse of my father when we arrived at the port was not of the crisp-uniformed, medal-bedecked war hero I had hoped to see standing alongside a mighty battleship. Instead it was of a bearded, disheveled man staggering out of a seedy-looking tavern. No ships. No parade of soldiers. No banners yet waving.

Dad quickly passed out in the car and slept for most of the trip home. The rest of us were mostly quiet, speaking in whispers, if at all, as though our red Valiant were the lone car in a funeral procession.

As it turned out, Dad's return from his stint in the merchant marine sounded the death knell for life as we knew it. The insurance firm he had previously worked for refused to rehire him, and three months later we were packing to leave the wonderful old house on York Road, following Dad back to Grand Rapids, where he was able to find another job as an insurance inspector. Barbara, who had graduated second in her class at Nazareth Academy, had to forfeit a scholarship that had been awarded to her by John Carroll University in the Cleveland suburb of University Heights. Mom had to say good-bye to her many aunts, uncles, and cousins in the Cleveland area. And I was shattered. I couldn't imagine leaving my friends and the school where, despite Sister Judith, I had felt so unconditionally accepted.

5. Uprooted

The house that Dad bought for us on the largely blue-collar, predominantly Polish west side of Grand Rapids was smaller than, though somewhat similar to, our house on York Road. But it had no pear trees out front, and the backyard offered barely enough space to play badminton, to say nothing of baseball. There was no beveled glass on the windows, so there were no rainbows to illuminate the interior of the house.

As for Dad, his trip to Vietnam seemed only to have intensified his own internal darkness. In the engine room of a troop carrier he had discovered the body of a young Army draftee who had hung himself. In Da Nang he had come face-to-face with the blind, limbless, and napalm-disfigured victims of the war—children as well as young U.S. soldiers. He would graphically recount these horrors during his drunken rages. He no longer watched the nightly news.

Angry and resentful at my forced departure from a place I had loved, I distracted myself by focusing my attention on schoolwork, making new friends, and following my theatrical interests. My new school was Sacred Heart, only five blocks from our house on Hovey Street. A large red-brick building, it

was in many respects very similar to Holy Family School, and it, too, had mandatory morning Mass. It was a refuge from a home life made miserable by my father.

I was assigned to a class that included both seventh- and eighth-graders, watched over by a charming, funny, and dedicated teacher known as Sister Mary Tarsicia. She divided her attention between the two grade levels—a task that many other teachers probably would have found difficult. Schoolwork came easy for me, and it didn't take me long to prove myself as a fairly bright kid. When it came to speaking up in class, I wasn't shy. In fact, I was something of a show-off. I'd often sworn that I'd never be like my father, but I could see that some of his characteristics—at least his pride of intellect—were beginning to emerge in me.

I was eager to adjust at Sacred Heart. I tried out for the school football team and won a spot as a second-string receiver. I wrote a couple of plays that several of my classmates and I were allowed to perform for the class. I was also forming new friendships with both boys and girls, and soon I was feeling pretty good, the way I had back at Holy Family. With one major exception.

His name was Charlie Larsen, and he was an eighth-grader in Sister Mary Tarsicia's class. He wasn't an academic standout, but he was clearly one of the most popular boys at Sacred Heart, with his dark eyes, thick hair, and squarish, strong-looking face. He was the starting quarterback for the Sacred Heart Falcons and a star forward on the basketball team. The school's cutest girls fawned over him, and his following of male friends included the jocks and the kids who constituted what I thought of as the school's hoodlum faction—the tough guys who swore, smoked cigarettes, and made fun of the teachers, priests, and other kids. For reasons that I never understood, Charlie Larsen did not like me, and he seemed intent on undermining everything I did.

6. Initiation

At first, Charlie came across as one of those charming teasers whose little barbs reflect an attitude of "Hey, no harm intended. Just kidding around." So I tried to be good-natured and put up with his seemingly lighthearted insults about my skinny legs and my hair, which I wore combed straight back with a little dab of Brylcreem. But as the year progressed, his insults grew more hostile, and—worst of all—he recruited other kids to assist in his hazing of me. Eventually, I couldn't walk down the hall without someone calling out, "Hey, Greaser!"

Hoping to shake that epithet, I changed the way I combed my hair and stopped using Brylcreem. But it was too late. The moniker stuck, and with several variations. I was Grease, Greaser, Greaseball, Grease-for-Brains. Then, not long before school let out for the summer, Charlie told some of his cohorts he had seen me in the locker room putting grease on my ass. Though the implication was unclear to me at the time, the remarks caused me no end of humiliation and misery. I started getting into fistfights. I wanted to tell somebody—most of all my dad. But I was afraid of what his reaction might be, so I quietly agonized, utterly isolated.

One day about a week before summer vacation started, I was standing on the school playground during recess, talking with Bobby LaPeer, an altar boy and aspirant to the priesthood. He was a smart, nice kid—one of only a few who had remained friendly with me. Having occasionally been the target of Charlie's insults, he probably felt some sense of camaraderie with me.

As Bobby and I stood talking, I suddenly felt an arm around my shoulders and heard Charlie's loathsome voice next to my ear. "Listen, Grease," he hissed, "I got something for you."

Big, fat Ted Lipski and a couple of other eighth-grade hoodlums had gathered around me by this time. Bobby, suddenly, was nowhere in sight.

"You seem pretty uptight lately," Charlie said in a tone of feigned concern.

"Yeah," chimed in Ted, "he got into another fight last week."

"Another fight!" Charlie moaned sarcastically. "You need something to calm you down, Greaseball, and I've got just the thing right here." He extracted a pack of Camel cigarettes from the pocket of his blue uniform slacks and held it before my eyes. "Ever smoke a cigarette before?" he asked.

A lot of the other kids on the playground had paused in the midst of their various activities and were now quietly eyeing us, watching the fast-developing scene. Knowing that I was no match for Charlie or any of his cohorts—let alone all of them—I was, of course, terrified. So I took the only course of action that seemed available to me. Charlie had loosened his grip on my shoulders when he pulled out the pack of cigarettes, and that allowed me to free myself, at which point I took off running as fast as I could, making a beeline for home. But I wasn't fast enough for the school's star athlete. With big, fat Ted lumbering behind him, Charlie tackled me on a lawn at the edge of the sidewalk that ran alongside Garfield Street. Flipping me over on my back like a helpless insect, he sat on my stomach, squeezing the breath out of me as he grabbed both my wrists and pinned my skinny arms above my head. I could feel the hot, stinging tears rolling down my cheeks.

"Hey, look at this, Ted," Charlie panted. "Greaseball's crying!"

His sidekick knelt down, breathing hard, and leaned over me. I could feel his noxious breath on my face. "Jeez, he is crying, Charlie," he said. "And we're just trying to be friends."

Three or four other boys had followed the chase, and by this time they were gathered on the sidewalk nearby. "Like I said"—Charlie said grinning wickedly—"you need to calm down, Ray."

He had never called me by my name before. Relative to everything else I was feeling, it was a vaguely pleasant surprise. I felt a slight sense of relief.

Ted shook a cigarette from Charlie's pack. Lighting it with a match he struck on the sidewalk, he took a few puffs. "Yeah, this does calm ya down," he said. "Don't it, Charlie?"

"Why don't you let Grea—I mean Ray have a drag or two, Lipski? He needs it."

Ted stuck the cigarette between my lips, and I drew several

puffs of smoke. The other boys grinned and chuckled as I coughed and mildly protested that I'd had enough. Charlie took the cigarette, examined it closely, and announced, "Hey, the kid didn't even nigger-lip it!" He took a drag while the others laughed some more, then he pulled me to my feet and brushed off the back of my white shirt.

"Looks like you've got a bit of a grass stain, Grea— I mean Ray. Sorry about that."

Relieved to be on my feet again, I laughed along with them. Then we all walked back to school. I entered Sister Mary Tarsicia's class with Charlie, his arm around my shoulders. I was quiet, thinking I'd just passed a test that would initiate me into the peer group whose acceptance I desperately craved. The taste of the cigarette was still strong in my mouth.

Grand thoughts ran through my head for the rest of the afternoon. It would be an immense relief, I thought, to no longer be the target of the abuse that had been heaped on me by Charlie and his pals. At the same time, I considered their world. They smoked cigarettes. They seemed to scorn good grades. They used the foulest language I had ever heard, and they made fun of things that I had always held in high esteem, like priests, teachers, and school plays. I looked over at Charlie, at his desk. He was whispering into the ear of Sandy Malinowski, the cute, blond cheerleader who sat in front of him. She was blushing and giggling with delight. Reconsidering the cigarette-smoke taste that lingered in my mouth, I decided I might be able to get used to it.

• • •

7. Misadventures of a Lost Youth

As I had hoped, my eighth-grade year at Sacred Heart brought an end to the insults and the hazing. Charlie Larsen had graduated, but I had gained acceptance among his friends. I learned to smoke and swear with the best—or worst—of them, and my grades dropped to about a C average. Most of my after-school time was spent hanging with the gang in front of a drugstore not far from school. We talked about cars and girls, and we made fun of the school sissies—the guys who were good students and showed respect for the teachers and priests, as I had once done. When my seminary-bound former friend Bobby LaPeer walked by, I joined in the chant "LaPeer's a queer, LaPeer's a queer!" Not that I felt good about it, but I did it anyway, because I couldn't bear the alternative. I needed to feel acceptance, and if that required betraying a friend—or my own identity—then that's what I had to do. At my eighth-grade graduation ceremony, Sister Mary Tarsicia gave me a look of quizzical concern, as if asking, Where have you gone?

It was a question that would haunt me for years to come.

Like Sister Mary Tarsicia and probably others, my parents hadn't been oblivious to the changes I'd been going through since the seventh grade at Sacred Heart. Reasoning that a geographic change might help the situation, they sold our house and bought a new one, complete with a swimming pool, near Allendale, ten miles west of Grand Rapids, in the country. That meant entering a new school, Grandville High, so I was once again the new kid.

Over the previous year and throughout the summer before entering high school, I'd let my hair grow. As the new kid out in the boonies, I was immediately tagged with the nicknames Hippie and, of all things, City Slicker. It was 1968, the year Richard Nixon—one of the politicians my father most despised—was elected president. Draft cards and bras were being burned in ever-increasing numbers, and legions of young people were hearkening to Timothy Leary's message "Turn on, tune in, drop out." In a weird, convoluted, adolescent way, I became one of America's lost youth.

I began drinking as often as I could during this period. I ran away from home every chance I could get, sleeping in garages or in old cars that friends were fixing up. I befriended almost anyone who was willing to hang out with me, and my only thoughts of school were connected to the truancy notices that my parents frequently received. My dad had taken to calling me a bum and a drug addict, and my mom defended me. They blamed each other for what I had become. My home life was worse than ever, and the cries of "You loser!" became so frequent that it felt like that was my new name.

During one of my runaway episodes, I met a girl named

Tracey. I was fourteen, a little more than six months out of parochial school, and although I feigned sexual knowledge, my experience with girls had been limited to holding hands on the local ice-skating rink and a few awkward attempts at kissing. I met Tracey on an illicit visit to Union High, the school I would have been attending had Mom and Dad not moved us from Hovey Street. Tracey was a sophomore there, and she rescued me from near-certain apprehension by the school authorities when she found me, half drunk on cough syrup, stumbling around the hallways in search of old friends from Sacred Heart. A tall, blond, tough-looking girl who wore dark eye makeup and bright red lipstick, she grabbed me and pulled me into the girls' bathroom. In rather earthy terms, she asked me what I was doing and advised me to leave the premises before a teacher or monitor saw me and called the cops. When I explained that I had nowhere to go, she suggested that we walk over to her Mom's house.

Tracey was a take-charge kind of girl, a year and a half older than I. When we arrived at her small bungalow, she explained that her mother was at work, so we could hang out there for the rest of the day, listening to music and drinking a few beers. She sat me in the living room and fetched two cans of Pabst Blue Ribbon beer. Then she put a Jimi Hendrix album on the hi-fi and lit some incense.

Within a few minutes there was a knock at the back door. Tracey abruptly shut off the music and extinguished the incense, then whispered sternly that if it was the cops or a truant officer, I had better sneak out the front door and make a run for it. Paranoia-stricken, I moved toward the door, prepared to make a hasty exit, while Tracey checked the back. A moment later she returned to the living room with a short, red-haired girl whom she introduced as Kim, a junior from Central High. The two of them began laughing and talking as if I weren't there, so I excused myself to get another beer from Tracey's mother's well-stocked supply in the kitchen. When I returned to the living room, Tracey was shuffling a deck of cards. "Wanna play some strip poker?" she asked.

After a moment's hesitation, I masked my total disbelief by adopting the tone of the man of the world I imagined myself to be. "Yeah, for sure," I said enthusiastically. "It's my favorite game."

Tracey turned the music back on, and we moved to the kitchen table. Kim offered me a cigarette, which I accepted. We played several hands of cards, discussing nothing else. Each time one of us removed an article of clothing, the girls giggled. Once both of them had shed their bras, I couldn't keep myself from staring. I had never seen a girl's breasts before, except in magazines, and I could feel myself blushing. Crossing and uncrossing my bare, gangly legs under the table, I was as embarrassed and frightened as I was aroused.

Suddenly Kim gave me a strange look. "You know, Tracey, this isn't quite fair," she commented, still staring at me.

"What isn't fair?" asked Tracey.

"Well, lover boy here is getting an eyeful. But what's in this for us?"

The girls shared a brief, malevolent glance, and I felt a new, threatening dynamic fill the small kitchen. In an instant, Kim reached under the table, snatched up my clothes, and threw them into the next room, shouting, "Free-for-all!"

Tracey shrieked with laughter, moved quickly toward me, and planted a mocking, wet kiss on my forehead. Aghast, I stood up, my thoughts and feelings momentarily trapped in a maze of new, terrifying stimuli. I wanted my clothes back, but the girls were blocking my way and pushing themselves up against me. I stumbled, and as the two pinned me to the floor, I fought back an instinctive urge to strike back. Hitting or fighting with girls was contrary to all I had learned in my years at Catholic school, and to everything my mother had taught me about how to treat young ladies. I shouted and tried to wriggle free, but my awkward squirming and helpless protestations only seemed to feed their delight. So I gave up my struggle.

"Very well, then," I said in a manner so cool and relaxed that it surprised even me. "Take me. Do what you will."

At that, Tracey and Kim suddenly stood up, freeing me. "Aw, you're not fun," Kim pouted. As they retreated up the stairs, Tracey scowled and commanded, "Get your things and leave."

More embarrassed and confused than ever, I quickly dressed and left. My attempts to unravel the meaning of this strange, provocative encounter with the public-school girls would fuel my adolescent imagination for a long time to come.

8. ULTIMATUM

Hungry, dirty, and smelling of sweat from two or three days of wandering, I pounded at the back door of my parents' house. It was early April 1970, less than a month after my sixteenth birthday. I hadn't made it home for the special dinner my mom had said she was going to make for me. The midafternoon sun felt unusually hot. My dad opened the door just as I was about to pound on it again. I hadn't expected to find him home at that time of the day, but there he was—calm, sober, and dressed for business in a white shirt and tie, holding a cup of coffee. Greeting me with a warm, compassionate smile, he stood in the doorway and looked up at the sun.

"It's springtime," he declared. "A time of new beginnings, and also time to take the storm windows off." Returning his gaze to me, he suggested, "Why don't you come in and take a bath."

This was the other dad—not the raging, frustrated nocturnal drunk, but the wise, sunny-dispositioned dad who spoke to us articulately, sometimes almost poetically. This was the dad who could fix nearly anything, from a bicycle sprocket to a transistor radio, who laughed uproariously at the simplest of life's absurdities and could answer any homework question with authority and intelligence. Because we desperately wanted this dad in our lives, we tolerated his counterpart, who humiliated and terrorized us.

Fifteen or twenty minutes after he opened the door for me on that memorable spring day in the early stages of my sixteenth year, I entered the kitchen, freshly showered and wearing clean clothes. Laid out on the counter before me were ham, cheese, and bread from the refrigerator. Dad invited me to make myself a sandwich and join him at the table.

When I sat down with my sandwich, he didn't bother to grill me about my whereabouts over the last several days. Instead, he adopted a matter-of-fact tone as he said, "You need to make a decision, Ray. You're not in school anymore, though I wish you were. You need to be doing something with your time and your life—something other than hanging out with your friends, as you say."

I silently contemplated his words as I chewed on my sandwich, and he continued. "Your mother and I have discussed this at some length, and it comes down to a simple ultimatum: You must either get back into school or get a job. The only other alternative is that you leave this house—not for a two- or three-day romp, but permanently. We love you, but it's time to make some serious choices."

I sat there considering several other alternatives. Part of me wanted to toss aside the remainder of my sandwich and fly out the door in yet another act of defiance. Another part of me felt like calling my dad on his drunken, abusive behavior and the agony he'd caused our family. But I was so exhausted at the pointlessness of my existence, and so ashamed of the pain I knew I had caused my mom and even him. Tears began to well up in me just as my mom returned from her job at the library of Grand Valley State College. She was already crying as she came over to the table.

"Oh, Ray, we love you so much," she said.

That was all it took to bring the three of us into a tearful embrace.

9. GAINFULLY EMPLOYED

The silver-haired woman at the unemployment bureau slid her bifocals down her nose and studied me. I had spent the morning taking a battery of tests to measure my intelligence and manual dexterity, and she had just finished evaluating the results. The scene reminded me of sitting in the guidance counselors' office at school.

"You did very well on all the tests, young man," she told me. "I can't help but wonder why you're not in school. You were obviously a good student."

"Yes, ma'am, thank you," I said confidently. "But high school really turned me off."

"I see," she responded. "Well, be that as it may, the situation is this: You're a bright, young fellow, but you're also a high-school dropout, and you have no employment history."

Her pronouncements stung, and the word *dropout* filled me with shame.

"There is an opening, however," she added. "What do you think of working as a busboy?"

That question perked me up. "A busboy!" I repeated, thinking that she must have read the section of my application where I listed travel as one of my main interests. I imagined myself sitting alongside the driver of a Greyhound or Trailways bus. I figured I'd probably be doing a little sweeping of the aisle and maybe handing out pillows to passengers, like the ground-travel equivalent of a flight attendant.

"Yes!" I responded enthusiastically. "I'd love to be a busboy!"

The lady seemed as delighted as I was. She wrote a name and address on a piece of paper and handed it to me. "See Mr. Bob Roggow at the Woodland Mall," she instructed. "Mr. Fables Family Restaurant."

I pocketed the piece of paper and thanked her. "A busboy!" I repeated to myself again. But, I wondered, why was I meeting this man at a restaurant? Maybe I'd be on some mall commuter bus—a prospect that didn't sound nearly as adventurous as traveling around the country on a Greyhound. Oh well, I figured, at least I'd be cruising around, and probably meeting a lot of girls. Cool, I thought.

A few days later I was standing in the dining room at Mr. Fables Family Restaurant, wearing a white shirt with a black bow tie, my hippie hair neatly trimmed to an Ivy League cut, holding a plastic tub under one arm and a damp towel in the opposite hand. I was a busboy.

I quickly realized that being a busboy was a job with zero prestige. Sometimes, as I dutifully moved around the restaurant, clearing tables and wiping under salt and pepper shakers, I reflected wistfully on my glory days as president of my sixth-grade class back in Parma Heights. "I'm a busboy," I repeated to myself, sadly. Despite the sense of humiliation—an all-too-familiar feeling—I managed to convince myself that I could work my way up the corporate ladder at Mr. Fables. That thought gave me some encouragement as I repeatedly backed my way through the swinging doors to the kitchen, both hands gripping my heavy bus tub full of dirty dishes, silverware, glasses, and garbage.

I threw myself body and soul into my lowly job, and within a month Mr. Roggow bumped my salary up by a dime an hour. When he told me about the raise, I felt as if I'd been promoted to chief executive. In my mind I became Super Busboy, and by the time summer rolled around, I was in charge of the barrel, as the kitchen's dishwashing area was known.

Over the following year I adopted the goal of becoming a crew manager at the restaurant. I learned all I could about every aspect of the business, from dishwashing and back-room setup to managing the cash register and keeping the inventory, and eventually I spoke to Bob about my prospects for a crew manager's job.

"You're a good worker, Ray," he told me. "But the company has a policy that crew managers have to have a high-school diploma."

I was crushed. I went home and got drunk with my dad, both of us bemoaning our miserable fates.

Mom, ever the wise and practical one, had a simple suggestion: "Go to night school." So I did. I attacked my studies as voraciously as I had gone about my work at the restaurant, and in less than a year I'd earned the right to take my graduate equivalency diploma test.

Dad still drank heavily and relentlessly lamented his past, but in the weeks leading up to the test, he drilled me night after night in math, science, and English. Sometimes he would wake me in the wee hours of morning, always with a glass of wine in his hand, and ask me to conjugate a verb or recite a mathematical formula. Such episodes would typically serve as a prelude to strange and lengthy philosophical diatribes.

"Conjugate the verb *be* in the future perfect tense," he would command, adding, "*Be,* as in 'To be or not to be?'— the issue of the ages. 'O death, where is thy sting?' "

On the morning of the exam, he was stone sober as he drove me to take the test. Quietly, he wished me good luck. He had tears in his eyes.

10. FATHER RAY

In late October 1972, I was in my freshman year at Thomas Jefferson College. Although I was enrolled in a bachelor of philosophy program, I focused most of my energy on the theater, studying set design, construction, lighting, makeup, directing, and, of course, acting. For the first time since seventh grade, I was involved in theater again. The play was *The Trial of the Catonsville Nine,* Daniel Berrigan's antiwar drama about the legal proceedings brought against him, his brother Philip, and seven other activists for their destruction of draft records in a Maryland office of the U.S. Selective Service System. I had been cast in the role of David Darst, one of the defendants, and my costume consisted of a dark suit and a black shirt with a clerical collar. Bill Hill, who played the part of the judge, invited me to a Halloween party.

"What should I wear?" I asked him.

"Just come as you are," he suggested. "I'll introduce you as Father Ray. I'm sure that by the end of the evening you'll be hearing confessions and performing the Benediction."

Thus did I meet the occupants of what was known as Ogre House, a two-story, five-bedroom communal house in a neighborhood populated mostly by students and other people in their twenties.

The Ogres were a motley crew: Vietnam veterans, young professionals, leftovers from the flower-power movement, academics, musicians, actors, and a librarian. The common threads that held the group together were a lust for partying and a general enthusiasm for sports. We would get together for Sunday-afternoon baseball games. Statistics were carefully tabulated for every player, and evenings often found the official Ogre House statisticians comparing notes and arguing over games from years gone by.

Regular attractions at Ogre House included theme and costume parties, Ogres in Action slide shows, and film festivals, usually featuring old Buster Keaton or Keystone Kops comedies. It was rare to find nothing happening there, so I made a habit of stopping by almost every night. Even on the occasional dull evening, I could be assured of finding someone to drink with.

My favorite Ogre excursions were trips to attend the University of Michigan Wolverine football games. Several of us

would pack ourselves into a van on Saturday mornings for the two-hour drive to Ann Arbor. Lubricating ourselves with generous quantities of beer, we made sure that by the time we arrived in Ann Arbor, we were adequately tuned for the game and related activities.

For sheer numbers and concentrated human energy, there was nothing in my experience that could compare to a packed Michigan Stadium during football season. David Hunsberger—a fellow Ogre, brilliant theatrical performer, and my roommate for a while—would stand on his seat throughout the games. As the other fans shouted, "Let's go, Blue!" he would scream, "Woodstock had nothing on this!!"

The Maize and Blue. The best college football. Electricity!

I loved those trips to Ann Arbor. In those days it was known as Cerebral City and the Berkeley of the Midwest. The community offered an intoxication of its own.

My theater work at Thomas Jefferson also harmonized nicely with my social life. At Stage III, the college's experimental theater space in downtown Grand Rapids, I worked in various capacities on productions of Shakespeare, Chekhov, Beckett, Pinter, and Neil Simon, as well as student-written plays. It was a program of study that invited a great deal of socializing, which, in turn, seemed to require a great deal of drinking.

My drinking sessions with fellow theater enthusiasts often took place at any of several college hot spots, most notably the White Rabbit and the Eastown Saloon, two of my favorite haunts. Both were located on Wealthy Street, which—ironically enough—ran through the heart of Grand Rapids' black ghetto.

The White Rabbit, named for a Jefferson Airplane song from the late sixties, was a rock 'n' roll jukebox dive with Alice-in-Wonderland decor, and it was packed almost every night of the week. Among my more memorable experiences there was the night a group of us reenacted the old Robert Service ballad "The Shooting of Dan McGrew"—a spontaneous event that I narrated. The performance won our large table a hearty ovation and several rounds of free drinks.

Six or eight blocks up the street was the Eastown, which gained notoriety when the California country-rock sound became popular in the mid-1970s. The local bands that performed there regularly covered songs by the Eagles, the Flying Burrito

Brothers, Jimmy Buffett, the Charlie Daniels Band, and the Allman Brothers Band. Guys who frequented the Eastown generally wore blue jeans, leather vests, cowboy boots, and cowboy hats, and the place had a small dance floor, where the nimble of foot—as well as the not so nimble, including yours truly—shuffled around in myriad varieties of the Texas two-step. My stage performer's instincts inevitably overrode my abilities, and I imagined myself quite the rug cutter, not to mention ladies' man.

There seemed no end to the country-rock songs that celebrated and promoted heavy spirit consumption, and their lyrics provided ample justification for drunken stupidity, broken relationships, car wrecks, and the blackouts I was beginning to experience with increasing regularity. No matter what the occasion, nonoccasion, or calamity, there was a twangy ditty to assure me that drinking was the appropriate response.

Another appealing aspect of the country/cowboy style was that, good, bad, or ugly, the protagonist typically rode off into the sunset to lick his wounds, indifferent to the pain of those he left behind. It was a detached, macho attitude I longed to develop.

Drugs helped me do just that. By the time I was twenty-one, I had experienced the effects of a wide variety of illicit substances. In my early teens I had sniffed glue and experimented with LSD. I had eagerly consumed just about anything that was recommended to me as a good high—uppers, downers, mushrooms, pot. But nothing changed my life more—or did more to promote a feeling of total indifference to others—than cocaine.

11. COCAINE COWBOY

It was May 1976, and Grand Rapids was in the midst of an early heat wave. I was living in a house on Wellington Court, just a few doors down the block from Ogre House. My roommate, David, had left early for an acting workshop he was directing. Jeff Beck's LP *Blow by Blow* was playing on the stereo, and the girl I'd picked up at the Rabbit the previous night was still asleep in my bed as I swaggered down the stairs. Wanting to get a jump on the approaching weekend, I had decided to cut classes.

I grabbed a cold beer from the refrigerator, stepped out onto the front porch, and took a seat on the top step. I had been there for only a few minutes when the front door of the house across the narrow, one-way street opened and a dark-haired, sharp-nosed girl wandered out into the bright sunlight. I had seen her before, but we'd never been introduced. On that particular morning she was wearing cutoff blue jeans, platform shoes, and a tight black David Bowie T-shirt. I waved at her and shouted, "Howdy," and that was enough to bring her clomping across to our front porch.

"I'm Katie. Nice day, ain't it?" she said and sat down next to me.

"My name's Ray," I responded. "Good day for drinking."

"Like any day isn't." She laughed.

Katie and I were clearly destined for friendship. There ensued a conversation about music, mutual acquaintances, and getting drunk. She mentioned that she was planning to spend the weekend at a friend's house while he was away on business, and she spontaneously invited me to join her.

"It's on a lake, about an hour north of town. I've got money and beer."

Ten minutes later I was climbing into her '68 Mustang convertible and lying to her about how much I liked Bowie's music, too.

The tiny cottage on Long Lake smelled of smoke from the small woodstove, and the decor consisted largely of furniture that looked as if it came from cheap secondhand shops or yard sales. There was, however, a state-of-the-art stereo system with a huge collection of record albums. The place was also equipped with two Smith & Wesson handguns—one of which we found lying out on the kitchen table and the other tossed casually on the floor—not to mention dozens of boxes of .38-caliber bullets stacked in various places.

The one nice piece of furniture in the house was a luxurious four-poster bed; it was crowded into the bedroom along with a dresser, which held a chemist's scale, a telephone, and an assortment of hash pipes. Alongside the dresser was a large plastic garbage can that I soon discovered was filled with Mexican herb. Katie joked about her friend's pharmaceutical import business, high-speed chases, and occasional shoot-outs with competitors in Detroit. I laughed along with her, but the joviality was forced, and I felt an unspoken impulse to make up some excuse to get back into town. It didn't calm me down when Katie suggested that we go out back and blow off a few rounds with the .38. But I managed to convince myself that this was merely a cool adventure, a weekend drunk during which Katie and I would no doubt be rocking that four-poster bed a few times. Because I lived for just such thrills, I stifled any inclinations toward discretion as I guzzled another beer and loaded six rounds into one of the Police Specials.

We had been taking turns shooting at cans, bottles, and fence posts when Katie announced that she was going to the house to "take a whiz and get a couple more beers." I reloaded the gun and took a few more shots; then I heard her hollering for me to come inside. I found her sitting at the small kitchen table opening a sandwich bag that contained about a tablespoon of white powder.

"Ever do this before?" she asked in a peculiarly derisive tone.

"What is it?" I inquired.

"Coke, you ninny," she shot back at me.

"Yeah, a few times," I lied. "Never impressed me too much."

"You never did it my way," she said as she opened a chromium-plated cigarette case and removed a hypodermic syringe. "Want to give it a try?"

"Sure," I whispered nervously.

Katie immediately pulled a spoon from a kitchen drawer and, using a corner from a small piece of paper, scooped some of the powder into the spoon. "Get me a glass of water," she said, pointing to a cupboard. "And tie this bandanna around your arm," she added, tossing me a red handkerchief that had been lying on the table.

I placed the glass of tap water on the table and watched as Katie drew the liquid up into the syringe, rinsing it several times and shooting the water across the room like thin squirt-gun blasts. Then she drew up a measured amount with the syringe and shot it into the spoon. The powder immediately dissolved. A distinctive chemical smell rose into the air, and Katie seemed to momentarily relish it. A small wad of cigarette filter was the next thing she added to the spoon. Then she drew the liquid contents through it. "This shit looks very clean," she whispered. "Ready?"

With that I held out my arm.

"You've got great veins," she said.

A moment later I felt a sharp prick as the needle broke through my skin and entered a blood vessel. I watched as she drew a tiny mushroom of red into the syringe and then eased the plunger down. An instant later, the chemical smell that I'd noticed only seconds before seemed to permeate my entire mouth. My heart began racing and an electrical storm flooded my brain. Every grand moment of exhilaration that I'd ever known grabbed hold of my senses as I took deep, repeated breaths. My crotch got warm, and it felt like the wave of heat was rising through my entire body. It was the most sensual feeling I'd ever experienced compounded a hundred times over. It made me feel godlike in the twinkling of an eye. I grabbed Katie and planted a hard, open-mouthed kiss on her mouth and then fell away, rolling on the floor in pants and groans of total ecstasy.

My life would never be the same again. I fell in love with cocaine. That little hollow needle—which I had previously viewed with mild fright, as the source of unpleasant sensations experienced in the doctor's office—became the focal point of my existence. I had gone to the cottage on Long Lake a budding alcoholic. I left as a full-blown cocaine junkie.

I never returned to college that spring. Every waking hour found me scheming to make a quick buck to buy my new drug of choice. I used all manner of false pretenses to borrow money from my parents. I sought out other users who might supply me with a fix. I even tried my hand at selling coke in order to finance my own habit, but that approach invariably resulted in my shooting up the investment as well as the hoped-for profit. I lost all interest in everything I had formerly treasured—school, the theater, Sunday baseball games. Old friends stopped seeking out my company, and I became persona non grata even at Ogre House. I didn't care.

Over the next few years I struggled with my addictions to both cocaine and alcohol. Drunken binges sometimes found me warming the benches in local police holding cells, with no idea how or why I'd ended up where I was. I would tell myself, as well as others, that I didn't have a problem. Nothing anyone said about my behavior, or even my appearance, left anything but a passing impression on me.

My cocaine abuse would often culminate in tremors and convulsions. I hated who I was and regularly despised what I was doing. On numerous occasions I twisted the points off syringes, vowing to stop using, but moments later I would be digging through the trash to find them and carelessly "welding" the dulled tips back onto the plastic syringes with lit matches. Then I would worm the carpet with my fingers, trying to retrieve flakes of cocaine that might have fallen to the floor. There was more dirt and carpet fuzz than drug in these fixes. I would cry and wail when my brain failed to register a chemical rush. The degradation I heaped upon myself was immense.

Somehow, after a lengthy and largely oblivious hiatus from life and academia, I managed to finish my senior year at Thomas Jefferson. But there was no joy, or any of the fanfare that usually accompanies the receipt of a college degree. I became an emotional and sexual wanderer, bouncing around from one lukewarm relationship to another. Dad died.

12. Rehab and Relapse

As the 1970s were grinding to a halt, I met a young woman who seemed devoted to me and determined to change me for the better. Gretchen was a student at a local college. She and I were introduced at a rather low-key party and we struck up a friendship that soon evolved into romance. Although family and friends on both sides clearly had misgivings about the matter, we got married. Within three months, Gretchen was pregnant. I worked at odd jobs and joined Alcoholics Anonymous. Sue was born in August 1981.

Because I loved our daughter and wanted to be a father she could be proud of, I intensified my involvement with AA and enrolled in a master of education program at my alma mater. We began attending church services as a family. People who had originally cast wary, suspicious eyes on my relationship with Gretchen began to ease their gaze. Gretchen was a stable, hard-working mother, and I was—ostensibly, at least—a reformed mate who had a mind only for family and career advancement. But in the back of my mind skulked a longing for my old, decadent lifestyle, with its familiar chemical crutches.

It started with slips, as they call them in AA. I began sneaking a few drinks behind Gretchen's back. I'd smoke a joint while she was at work. In a few months, I found myself spending some nights away from home and lying about my whereabouts. Time after time I returned home from my binges begging for forgiveness. But Gretchen was obviously growing weary of my habits. Although nothing was said about it, I could tell that she was becoming detached from me.

Shortly after our fourth anniversary, I left home for several days on the self-justifying pretext that I was searching for my true identity. I drank and consorted with the demons of my past, with a kind of nostalgic eagerness to embrace the false promises they offered. I concluded that I was incapable of being the perfect father I had dreamed of becoming. I was haunted by the words of condemnation my own father had spoken to me during my wayward adolescence: "You're a loser, Raymond. You're a zero!"

In a drunken stupor, I drove to our empty home, pulled a paring knife from a kitchen drawer, and carved open my wrist and arm.

I regained consciousness later that evening to find myself strapped to a bed in a seclusion room at a local hospital. I had survived my suicide attempt. But that was the end of my relationship with Gretchen and my vague hopes of being the perfect father to our daughter.

13. Downward Spiral

Little more than a year had passed since I'd landed in Middletown, Connecticut. I had retreated from Michigan in order to heal—to attend to the wounds of a failed marriage and to recover from years of addiction. I wanted to start my life anew, and to get it right this time. I joined a Christian Reformed church, got involved in a recovery group, and found a job as a substance-abuse counselor. I also started waiting tables part-time to help pay off bills left in the wake of my divorce. It was a hopeful but ultimately flawed plan, as weak as the short-lived sobriety I had enjoyed and been so confident about.

My relapse began easily enough, with sips from not-quite-empty wine bottles that customers had left on tables at the restaurant, or a beer with my fellow wait-staff members after a particularly busy night, or a few hits off a joint. Then came the cocaine. Within a week after snorting a couple of lines off the back of the toilet-tank cover in the men's room with one of the kitchen workers, I was consumed with a craving for more. Satisfying that craving proved to be almost effortless. My job, counseling addicts, supplied me with plenty of leads. It also introduced me to Cassie, a heroin addict, whose brother was one of my clients.

We met at his apartment and immediately discovered our common interest in getting high. I was pleased to learn that Cassie was well acquainted with places to cop dope. At the time of our first meeting, I was gainfully employed and even had a small savings account at a local bank. But that was soon to change, because ours was a union of people, circumstances, and desires that was doomed from the outset.

The first thing I lost was my counseling job. When I failed to show up for work for several days in a row after successive nights of heavy drug use, my employers had no trouble figuring out what was going on, and they summarily dismissed me. To make up for the lost income, I increased my shifts at the restaurant. But it soon became clear that work was getting in the way of copping drugs with Cassie.

One of our favorite haunts was Boston Square, which was typical of the housing projects we encountered everywhere we ventured. The buildings were tired and military looking in their uniformity, and the place was overrun with children and young adults hungry for something to occupy themselves with. There were basketball courts and unsupervised play areas, but the main activities tended to be using and peddling drugs.

Visiting Boston Square on a regular basis, we would sometimes cruise the project's traffic circle in search of a favored connection. Other times, although never at night, I'd park the car and we'd set out walking. On one such occasion, as we hurried back to the car after copping a gram of coke, we were approached by a young African-American boy. He couldn't have been more than nine or ten years old, but he knew what these two white people were doing on his turf. Hesitating only slightly, he held out two insulin syringes for our inspection.

"N-n-new," he stammered. "T-t-two for f-five dollars."

I looked at the boy's worn basketball shirt and met his wide-eyed gaze. For a moment I considered his surroundings and miserable circumstances, and I imagined the monumental challenges that he would undoubtedly encounter. In that brief moment, I longed to lift him up into my arms and save him. But I didn't want that feeling. So I reached into my pocket and found a five-dollar bill, and in a single movement he and I snatched the contents of each other's hands. Then, with Cassie in tow, I raced back to the Chevy to fix myself—to escape the pain that this kid with the works had made me face.

14. Copping Amerika

I quit my job as a waiter—simply walked out after a Friday lunch shift and resolved never to go back. That's when Cassie and I decided we were going to leave town and travel the country in pursuit of the high, wherever that search might take us. I drained my savings account, and we packed a few belongings. The next morning we made a quick visit to her grandmother's grave. Then we headed out on our twisted, ill-conceived drug binge—a project that, in a perverse homage to Kafka, we had dubbed Copping Amerika.

We'd made a drug buy at Boston Square on our way out of town, but by the time we crossed the state line we had already shot the entire supply into our veins. Maintaining a steady wine drunk for the rest of the day, we traveled a rather awkward route through rural New York and into Pennsylvania. Our plan was to look for the Philadelphia drug district, but before I realized it, we had overshot the interstate exit. Thus did we find ourselves navigating a twisting concrete bridge into Camden, New Jersey.

There was a starkness about Camden that seemed almost surreal after spending most of the day driving through the country. It was like entering a war zone. Virtually all the buildings we saw were boarded up or in states of dire disrepair, and the people who walked the streets looked as battle fatigued as their surroundings. When it came to buying drugs, Cassie was usually eager to approach anyone anywhere, but in this miserably blighted environment, even she kept checking to see that the car doors were locked. Although it was oppressively hot outside, she left her window almost completely rolled up. We both felt enveloped by fear and a sense of total antipathy.

After we'd driven ten or twelve blocks, neither the scene nor our sense of the place had changed in any favorable way. As we approached a red light at a four-way intersection, Cassie commanded me to turn right. The brick structures on all but one of the corners were in various states of demolition. At that point, I decided it was time to turn around and get the hell out of Camden.

That's when we saw him—a thin Hispanic boy stepping out of an alleyway. Cassie pointed frantically at him and shouted for me to pull over. When I obediently stopped within several feet of the guy, Cassie rolled down her window and summoned him to the car.

"What you need?" the teenager asked as he peered into the car.

"Some of the girl," Cassie whispered, in the terminology of the street.

From his pocket he extracted three greenish-tinted cellophane packets, each about the size of a postage stamp and containing roughly half a gram of cocaine. Cassie dickered with him over the price and questioned the quality of his wares. Finally she handed him six twenty-dollar bills.

"You come back if you like," he said with a smile.

Day after day we traveled, pitching a tent when we needed to sleep. Some nights we slept on the roadside in the car. We rarely ate anything, and as our money ran out, we argued. We argued over who would make the next call to an old friend to beg for money, or who would get the last scrapings from used packets of heroin or cocaine. Like animals, we cursed and threatened each other. After the occasional day without drugs, we would overload our syringes the next time we scored. I was regularly throwing up from the dope and the booze, and I nearly went into convulsions several times. The road we were on seemed to be leading us straight toward death.

Eventually we headed back to Connecticut, lured by the promise of a long-awaited disability check from a former employer. It never materialized. By this time we had burned all of our bridges when it came to borrowing money. In desperation—feeling and probably looking like the battle-fatigued denizens of inner-city Camden—we went into a large discount store and shoplifted a toy gun. Then we staked out parking lots, looking for easy marks. When we spotted one, I jumped into the victim's car, ordered them to drive, and then stole their money. In all, we netted barely enough money for a couple of highs.

15. BUSTED

"There ain't no Buck here!" I said and slammed the telephone handset down into its cradle.

"Who was it?" asked Cassie in a tired, nervous tone of voice.

"A guy who said he was with the phone company. But something about the call didn't sound right. I think there was a police radio in the background."

"Oh, quit being so damn paranoid," she piped back at me.

Maybe she was right, I thought. The endless, alternating doses of cocaine, heroin, and booze had made me afraid of everything, every move. I longed to feel simple happiness—a sense that everything was okay. I wanted my mom to stroke the back of my head and tell me I was fine—that it was all just a bad dream. I pulled a sweatshirt over my head and stepped out into the backyard of the house where we'd hidden and slept uneasily the night before, the home of a concerned acquaintance. In vain, I kept telling myself that somehow, today, we'd be saved.

A dark station wagon slowed down and pulled into the driveway. A man wearing mirrored sunglasses and a dark sport coat climbed out from behind the steering wheel and approached me, a clipboard in his hand.

"Mr. Materson?" he asked.

"Don't know him," I said.

Suddenly the small yard was swarming with police officers brandishing sidearms and shotguns. In an instant, a pair of handcuffs was clasped on my wrists.

"I don't know him," I thought to myself.

The hours that followed came like a staccato of jump-cut film clips from all the police movies and TV cop shows I'd ever seen. I was frisked, photographed, fingerprinted, interrogated, and stared at by strange characters. Some of them were police officers; others were jail inmates with whom I was sequestered in a variety of holding cells along the way. Meanwhile, my soul wandered through a maze of terrified thoughts and feelings until, finally, I simply felt numb. Numbness seemed like the safest state to be in under the circumstances, although my stomach churned and ached from the absence of alcohol or dope in my system.

Eventually the man who had initially approached me with the clipboard called me out of a cell where I'd been sitting for more than an hour with several other captives. Sweating profusely, I felt oddly glad to see him. He spoke softly, but with firmness and authority. He didn't use the kind of crass language I'd been hearing from the jail guards, but he was clearly respected. He reminded me of Father Benechek, a priest I had known years earlier, during my days at Holy Family School. Leading me into a small office, he removed the handcuffs from my wrists and directed me to sit down in a straight-backed wooden chair that, oddly enough, recalled the furniture at Holy Family. The panicked thoughts and fearful emotions I had recently managed to numb came flooding back. Overwhelmed with shame and guilt, I desperately attempted to unburden myself by giving a full confession, spilling my heart and guts into the father-detective's tape recorder. I wept bitterly and fervently longed for absolution, but it was not forthcoming.

"Confession, Ray, is good for the soul," pronounced the man in the sport coat as he summoned guards to come and take me away. It was the last time I saw him. Instead of feeling absolved and forgiven, I felt like a whore who had opened my heart to an unfeeling, strange bedfellow. It felt like the last, hideous insult along a gauntlet of humiliation.

"You confessed?" my fellow inmate asked me in an incredulous tone that immediately convicted me of the ultimate stupidity.

"Yeah," I mumbled. "It just seemed like the thing to do."

There were about twenty other men, mostly blacks and Latinos, sitting with me in the large holding tank at the Morgan Street Jail in Hartford. The man slouched next to me was a wiry, crazed-looking individual, heavily tattooed. Recognizing me as a junkie coming down, he offered me a drag on his cigarette.

"I never known anyone who helped themself by confessing," he said. "You looking at kidnapping and robbery. You going to prison. Yeah, that's what I'd say."

"How much time do you think I'm looking at?" I asked.

"Twenty, maybe forty years," he quickly responded. "Yeah, you going to prison for a good long time."

"What's it like?" I asked, trying to hide my shock.

Putting his mouth up next to my ear, he whispered, "It's nigger world up there. But I got some advice for you: Soon as you get there, you get yourself a shank, a blade. The bigger the better. First day they let you out of the house, you grab the first big nigger you see. Stick that blade right up to his throat. It'll get everybody's attention fast. Big as the nigger is, he'll be squealing. Then you start screamin'. You say, 'See this, see this! I'll kill this nigger! I'll kill anybody that messes with me! I don't care who you are, I'll kill you!' See, you got to earn their respect."

"Respect," I whispered back. "Yeah, I hear ya." I was terrified. I couldn't even remotely imagine being a player in the scenario my passing mentor had suggested, unless I was the one on the business end of the shank, as he called it. Then I thought about his other pronouncement—"Twenty, maybe forty years." He moved away from me as I began to visibly shake. I desperately needed an alternate plan.

I spent several days and nights in the crowded holding tank. Mattresses were dragged in every night, and we all slept on the floor. Meals were delivered in paper bags: cereal, fruit, and milk for breakfast; bologna sandwiches, fruit, and milk for lunch and dinner. Cigarettes were scarce, and more than one face was bloodied in fights over those precious commodities. After my alarming conversation with the skinny tattooed guy, I spoke to no one else except a doctor who did cursory examinations of everyone who was brought to the jail.

The doctor was squat and round, with white hair and wire-rimmed glasses. He peered into my eyes through them. There was a warmth about his gaze that I hadn't seen in another human face for quite a while. After a brief examination and some questions about my general health, he said, "I see you're thirty-three. You know, Jesus Christ died when he was thirty-three. He spent three days in the tomb, but then he was gloriously resurrected. Perhaps you, too, will gloriously rise up from death." Then he paused, his eyes fixed on me, and said, "Think about it."

As I was escorted back to the tank, I wanted to contemplate what the doctor had said, but I knew it would only bring tears to my eyes, and that was something I couldn't let happen. Besides, I had already tried to touch base with my religious upbringing. I had confessed. But, if anything, that had only lessened my chances for "rising up." So I let my mind flood itself with angry, hateful thoughts, and I began considering how I might escape.

Two nights later, I was brutally and intentionally kicked in the face as I slept. My assailant was a wild Jamaican man with long, dusty dreadlocks who had been bothered by my snoring. The doctor had me transferred to the county lockup.

16. Pipe-Cleaner Animals

Unlike Morgan Street, the Hartford County Correctional Center was a state-of-the-art detention facility. Steel doors were electronically controlled from inside seemingly impenetrable booths composed of metal and reinforced glass. Corridors and cell blocks were monitored with video cameras, and guards patrolled the premises around the clock. The place was entirely surrounded by towering fences topped with coils of gleaming razor wire.

The incident that had gotten me transferred there was described in my paperwork as a "fight." So I was placed in a small isolation cell in a security-risk section of the jail. Both of my eyes were black and badly swollen, and my skull had been slightly fractured. As if I needed further convincing that escape was my only option for survival, my court-appointed attorney visited me and, in view of my confession, held out little hope for my case. When I asked her about the likely length of the seemingly inevitable prison term, she assured me that it would be in the double digits. Whether that meant ten years or ninety-nine, she couldn't say.

Although escape from HCCC clearly wouldn't be easy, I quickly became obsessed with the possibility that I might accomplish it, and I wasted no time in studying the entire facility. Every time I was called off the cell block, typically to meet my public defender, I looked for flaws or deficiencies in security. I listened intently to other inmates when they occasionally shared stories about successful escapes. Such incidents had been few and far between, and apparently they had always involved in-

side or outside help. I had no one to assist me with any type of plan, and I dared not share my thoughts on the subject. Any attempt on my part to escape would obviously have to be a one-man operation.

The tedious routine at the jail was as predictable as the Mass service I had known as a child, and it gave no indication of any weakness in security. If I was going to escape, I decided, it would have to be while I was away from the facility. My public defender was preparing for the possibility that she might use my drug addiction as the basis for a diminished-capacity defense, so I had been making court appearances almost every other week—always, of course, under armed escort. Often I would go to court and spend hours in a holding cell, in leg shackles and resting on a steel bunk, only to be told at the end of the day that my case was continued. On such occasions, the only items in the cell with me were the contents of the brown-bag lunch that I had brought from the jail—fruit, milk, and a bologna-and-cheese sandwich.

During one such nonappearance at court, I opened my bag to discover that my sandwich was rather badly mashed. Instead of becoming angry, I was reminded of the communion hosts I had fashioned from the same kind of white bread during my make-believe turns as a priest in my childhood years. I noticed how the stem from the apple that was also in the bag had left a perfect impression in the doughy surface. Then I looked down at the leg shackles I was wearing. If I could make an imprint of the keyhole, I thought, I might somehow be able to fashion a key. Since the same keys were used to unlock both the shackles and the handcuffs used at HCCC, I knew that any reasonable facsimile could be my key to freedom. So I wadded up a small piece of bread and flattened it against the shackle, directly over the keyhole. When I carefully pulled it off, I was rewarded with a perfect impression. For the first time in months, I felt a small sense of victory. When the guards came back to my holding cell, I casually pocketed the piece of bread, feeling confident that it wouldn't be discovered when I was later frisked.

I was on my way to freedom.

"Court today?" asked Jimmy Jacoby as I was returning to my cell at HCCC that afternoon. Jimmy was a junkie, and one of the few fellow inmates I spoke with regularly.

"Yeah, just another wasted day," I said. Then, noticing the large brown grocery bag he was carrying at his side, I asked, "Commissary?"

"Yeah," he responded. "Not much in here neither. No candy. I'm jonesing, dude!" Laughing, he reached into the bag and pulled out a stick of deodorant. Holding it like a small pistol, he playfully jammed it into my ribs. "Give up the candy, punk!"

"Go ahead and shoot, white trash," I said in mock defiance. "You ain't gettin' nothing from me!"

As we shared a chuckle over our little exchange, the three o'clock head count was announced over the scratchy jailhouse intercom, and we headed back to our cells. "See ya at dinner," I called out to Jimmy over my shoulder.

Back in my cell, I quickly removed the miniature bread-dough cast from my pocket. I stifled a sinister laugh as a guard peered through the small window in my cell door.

"Materson!" he bellowed.

"Naaah," I sneered. "Santa Claus."

"No Christmas this year." He grinned through the opening. Then, continuing his walk up the tier, he laughingly added, "Or the next year, or the next, or the next. Ho, ho, ho!"

"Bastard," I muttered under my breath. "We'll see about that!"

I spent the next several days thinking of nothing but escape. The usual taunts from the guards and my vile fellow inmates only strengthened my resolve. I began making preparations for my eagerly anticipated self-liberation.

The batteries that the jail's commissary sold to power radios and small portable televisions were encased in stiff metal, and I used fingernail clippers to pry off one of these coverings. Twisting it into a thin tube, I was pleased to see that the end of it fit perfectly into the bread casting of the shackle keyhole. With a snip and a fold, I fashioned a tooth on one end, so that it corresponded to the shape of the key. So consumed was I with my developing escape plan that I began having a recurring dream about it. In the dream I would manage to free myself from handcuffs and shackles, then run down a road. But as I approached a crossroads, a police car would come careening toward me, and just as it was about to strike me, I would awaken in a panicked sweat. I worried that this dream experience might be some kind of premonition, but it didn't change my plans.

The next step in my scheme was more complicated. I needed a gun, or at least a convincing facsimile of one. It was my friend Jimmy Jacoby's stickup charade that spawned an idea. The plastic deodorant canisters issued by the commissary were roughly the size of a cigarette pack, and I reasoned that I could cut and reshape two of them to fashion something vaguely resembling a small semiautomatic pistol—a "Saturday-night special." Using my fingernail clippers to snip teeth into a blade made of battery casing, I fashioned a tiny metal saw, with which I would create this phony firearm. It proved to be a time-consuming task.

I worried that the guards might find my absence from the day room suspicious and that—even worse—they might actually see me working on my fake gun during their hourly checks of the cell block. To avoid being caught in the act, I always kept my back to my cell door, with its surveillance window, and I labored most feverishly during the minutes immediately after a guard had stopped to peer in at me. To further shield my devious craft, I devised a clever cover: I ordered pipe cleaners from the commissary and began intertwining them to create little pipe-cleaner animals, with which I decorated my cell. Some of them I suspended from a mobile that I attached to the ceiling. When I wasn't working on the "gun," I stashed the parts and my little homemade saw in the bottom of a box of Nilla Wafers, along with my homemade handcuff key. I told no one, not even Jimmy, about my doings. But two of the nosier inmates did ask me to make pipe-cleaner mobiles for their cells.

It took me nearly a month, working only in seemingly safe moments, to complete the production stage of my project. My cell was searched twice during that period, during routine block shakedowns. Because I was always polite and wasn't known to make trouble, the guards considered me a nice guy, and they were never very thorough in searching my little corner of the block.

17. Close Call

Christmas 1987 and New Year's Day 1988 passed uneventfully. My mother sent me a card and a money order, but I didn't reply. I also received cards from several people at the church I had joined in Connecticut. Instead of cheering me, these gestures from my well-wishers on the outside only saddened me and gave me twinges of guilt as I proceeded with my escape plans. But I refused to let guilt—or anything else—stand in my way.

By the end of January I had pieced my gun together. Lacking access to glue, I had used matches to partially melt the plastic parts so as to weld them to each other—a long, slow process that, on some of the more delicate joints, had to be repeated one or more times. But the nearly finished product pleased me. All that remained to be done was to paint it. Paint was as impossible to come by as glue, so I had to improvise, using an ear swab dipped in ink from the cartridge of a ballpoint pen. It was a sticky procedure, and it took days for the ink to dry. But finally the gun was complete.

Concealed in the bottom of the Nilla Wafers box, my make-believe weapon and homemade handcuff key gave me a feeling of power. I knew that was ludicrous, but it made me feel special. Not merely another hapless inmate in the hands of the cretin pawns that represented the criminal justice system, I was a force soon to be reckoned with.

"Break nineteen," came the loud call outside my cell. "Shakedown!"

It was early. The door rolled open to reveal two guards standing outside—an old-timer and a rookie. This was a bad combination, because even the more easygoing guards were apt to put on a show for the rookies they were assigned to educate. I smiled and greeted them with a "Good morning."

"Step out of the cell, please," said the tenderfoot.

"Materson here is a real desperado," the older man taunted. "Shoulda seen him when he got here—a real mess, eh Mattie?"

The new kid responded with an uncertain laugh and brusquely patted me down as I stood against the wall outside my cell. Removing a ballpoint pen from my pocket, he pulled the cap off of it and inspected it intently before handing it back to me. Then he took a position outside the door, watching his teacher with the innocent eagerness of the little boy looking through the toy-store window in the Norman Rockwell painting.

After several minutes, the search of my cell still in progress, I eased closer to the door so that I, too, could see what was going on in there. It was definitely *showtime* for the rookie. My mattress lay on its side, the bedding stripped and wadded on the floor, which was also strewn with letters, cards, notepads, and court papers. My mobile had even been pulled from the ceiling. My nervousness turned to fear as the senior guard grabbed my box of Nilla Wafers from the metal shelf where I stored my soap, toothpaste, and other commissary items. Knowing that I was done for if he were to open the box and pour out the contents, I had to take action.

"Sir," I said sheepishly, "did you see my collection of animals?"

"Ah, yeah, cute, Materson," he responded, holding on to the box of cookies. "Good that you can keep yourself busy."

"Maybe you saw the animals, sir," I offered as I nonchalantly stepped past the rookie guard and back into my cell, "But did you notice this?"

I reached out and picked two of the pipe-cleaner creations from the small desk-table that was bolted to the wall. Gently stroking the fuzzy wire figurines, I whispered to them, "Everything will be all right. There, there, you're okay.

"This is my monkey," I explained to the older guard as I held one of the things out before him in the palm of my hand.

"Yeah, yeah," he commented, giving me a nervously befuddled look. "Like I said, cute."

"And see how the monkey can sit on the elephant's back?" I continued, now holding both of the animals in front of the guard's face. "He likes you."

"You're nuts, Materson!" he blurted out. "You've freakin' lost it!"

Tossing the box of cookies aside, he backed quickly away from me and out the door. "Close nineteen," he shouted. "Nuts! A damn fruitcake," he muttered, walking off with his trainee in tow.

"Thanks, guys," I said to the animals.

LATE THAT EVENING, A PAPER was slipped under my door. It was a notice for my appearance at Hartford Superior Court the following day, February eighth. The close call with the guards that morning had convinced me that it was time to carry out my escape plan, and this outing would provide as good an opportunity as I was likely to get. I wasn't going to take any further risks of getting caught with my gun and handcuff key without even having had a chance to use them. And so I composed a script in my head, to be delivered at the moment I pulled my carefully crafted ink-painted deodorant-canister gun. I couldn't afford to stumble over my words or hesitate in making my intentions known. As in theater, to make my role and character believable, I would have to utterly command the space. I was nervous and afraid, but I remembered a pertinent bit of advice from a former college drama professor, Bob Moyer. If I was afraid, Bob had told me, I could make that fear work for me in the portrayal of my character.

Still, the fear kept me up later than usual. My night was restless and filled with vivid, disturbing dreams, in which I re-experienced my drug-addled journey with Cassie. My mind was filled with images of cocaine, syringes, and the ritual of getting high. At one point, breathing heavily and soaked in sweat, I awoke to find myself looking for a needle I was sure was still embedded in my arm. My stomach ached, and I felt as if I were once again going through the withdrawal that had consumed me during my first several days of incarceration. After managing to convince myself that I'd been dreaming, I slipped back into an uneasy sleep, only to find myself in another replay of my recurring escape dream. As always, I removed the handcuffs, then struggled with the shackles, finally freeing myself. I began running past buildings and road signs I couldn't read. Finally the familiar crossroads appeared, but I kept my pace up as the police car came screaming inevitably toward me. As it approached, I leaped into the air and soared over the top of it. Like a moonwalker, I landed softly, gently, and resumed my sprint. I was victorious, free.

18. Anywhere Next Exit

As I had the day before, I awoke to an early call outside my cell: "Break nineteen. Materson, you got court today. Shower. Get ready."

Despite my uneasy night, I felt rested and confident. My victorious resolution of the recurring escape dream seemed an omen that everything was coming together for me. I showered and dressed, feeling assured that I would soon be experiencing the freedom I had known in my dream. The guard who was to escort me to the jail's transportation section tossed the familiar lunch bag into my cell and asked whether I was ready.

"Just need to go to the bathroom," I lied.

"Okay," he responded. "I'll be back in a couple of minutes."

As soon as the guard turned away from my cell, I reached for my box of Nilla Wafers, removed my homemade pistol and handcuff key, and stashed them in the bottom of the lunch bag, under the bologna-and-cheese sandwich. Having accomplished that much, I gave some forethought to the routine ahead of me, fully realizing that my escape plan could be thwarted in any of several ways. During the obligatory pat-down search as I was about to board the transport van, my lunch bag could be inspected, although that had seldom happened in the past. The van might be very crowded, and inmates hoping to earn brownie points or breaks from the court might expose me as I removed my irons. The key might not work, or the guards might not fall for the phony gun. Although I worried about such possibilities, I clung tenaciously to my dream, mentally reliving my graceful victory leap over the screaming police car.

"I'VE GOT A TWENTY-EIGHT-CALIBER Colt ready to bore a hole in your head if you don't do exactly what I say!"

The guard in the passenger seat whipped his head around and looked at me through the steel grid that separated him and the driver from the inmates in the back of the Corrections Department van.

"Turn back around and put your hands up on the dash, or your partner is dead meat!" I screamed. "Do you hear me?! Do it!!"

The guard hesitated for a moment, but as I flashed the small makeshift gun in his direction, he moved his hands in compliance with my demand.

"What the hell's going on?" the driver asked anxiously.

"I think he's got a gun, Frank," the passenger guard sputtered.

"Where the hell did he get a gun?"

"Never mind where I got the gun!" I screeched with nervous excitement. "Just do like I tell you, and I won't have to hurt anybody. I don't want to hurt anyone, but I will if I have to! I got nothin' to lose!"

"Listen, man," the driver blurted out, "you need to think this thing out!"

"I have thought it out! I got AIDS, man, and I ain't going to die in prison!" I screamed back at him. It was apparently the right thing to say, because in the next breath he was asking me what I wanted them to do. My fellow inmates—two frightened-looking white kids—said nothing as the exchange proceeded.

I felt completely crazed at this point, and everything I said to the two worried guards came out in screams and frantic shouts. Adrenaline was coursing through me like a fresh shot of cocaine. I kept jerking the gun around menacingly, because I didn't want them to get a chance to study it. But it was more pure fear than acting technique that was fueling my performance.

"Get on the interstate, south!" I ordered.

I wanted to find Cassie. Since the arrest, I had received one sentimental, cartoon greeting card from my companion in crime. "Miss ya, Cassie," read the terse, handwritten note. There was no return address, but the envelope had been postmarked from Middletown. So that's where I decided to go. My plan was to find Cassie and resume our drinking-and-drugging binge. This time, I calculated, we would leave the East Coast and live like outlaws until the authorities forgot about us.

I watched the signposts shoot past as the van sped down I-91 on that heavily overcast winter day. At the Route 9 exchange, I directed the driver to head toward Middletown. I imagined how totally impressed Cassie would be when she saw that I had escaped. This time, I thought to myself, we would be untouchable. Maybe they could catch us, but they couldn't keep us. And we would be together for Valentine's Day.

The driver glanced back at me and asked, "Where should I get off?"

"Anywhere," I said, feeling myself briefly slip out of my harsh, sinister character. "Next exit!" I barked, regaining my equilibrium.

NO FEAR, read the decal on the rear window of a car that passed us.

19. F BLOCK

Restrained in leg irons and handcuffs, I stood in a Hartford courtroom, under the watchful eyes of two armed guards and a state trooper behind me. My attorney stood before the judge's bench pleading my case, which had not been helped by my attempted escape. To make a not-so-long story even shorter, I had been out long enough to track down Cassie at a friend's house, but when I showed up there, her friend's boyfriend promptly called the cops, who came over and rearrested me. My three hours of freedom—and my theft of ten bucks from the driver of the Corrections Department van—had added new counts of armed kidnapping, armed robbery, and attempted escape to the already weighty charges against me. There was little that could be said in my defense. A gray-haired man in his late fifties, the judge rifled through a stack of papers that the state's attorney had handed him. From time to time he glanced at me over the top of his reading glasses. After an interminable few minutes, he put the papers down and addressed the court.

"Though it appears to me that the charges against Mr. Materson add up to more than one hundred and fifty years of incarceration," he began, "I am willing to accept the state's plea arrangement. Therefore, I am remanding Mr. Materson to the custody of the Connecticut Department of Corrections for a period of twenty-five years, suspended after fifteen." Then, fixing his eyes directly on me, he said, "I hope, Mr. Materson, that this gives you sufficient time to reflect on your offenses. Consider yourself fortunate."

I left the courtroom feeling totally empty. I kept telling myself that I could relax now, that it was over. But I knew it wasn't. As I shuffled along behind one of my armed escorts, my public defender appeared at my side.

"You're pretty lucky, Ray," she said. "You'll make it. Stay in touch."

"Yeah, right," I sighed.

A few minutes later, as I rode with my escorts to the state prison in Somers, the guard in the passenger seat up front turned around and looked at me. Spinning the cylinder of the large-caliber, nickel-plated revolver he held in one hand, he chuckled. "Like the judge said, Materson, 'Consider yourself fortunate.'"

I did not, of course, feel in any way lucky or fortunate. I felt like the total loser my father had always told me I was. At the same time, I was consumed with anger—at my parents for bringing me up in a dysfunctional, alcoholic home; at my junior-high-school classmates for incessantly teasing and belittling me; at God and His church and its rules and empty promises of love and abundance; at Cassie, whom I held responsible for encouraging my drug abuse and criminal behavior; at the judicial system that had just sent me back to prison with a substantially extended term; and at this dumb armed guard who sat there mocking me. Most of all, though, I was infuriated with myself, sickened by the notion of a good boy gone bad.

Such were the thoughts in my head when the van arrived at the state prison. Gazing out the window at the guard towers and the tall fences, I could almost hear the sounds of the chains and banging steel doors inside. "A good boy gone bad," I thought. But as I surveyed the institution that was going to be my new home, evidently for quite some time, I was vaguely aware that there was a lonely, rejected part of me that had not gone bad.

"I DON'T MESS WITH NOBODY, and I don't want nobody messing with me" were the first words I spoke to fellow inmates at the Connecticut Correctional Institution in Somers. Shortly after my arrival I had been sent to shower. I had thought I might have the shower room to myself, but no sooner had I stepped under the water than two muscle-bound black inmates joined me. I was feeling very pale and vulnerable, but when neither of them responded to my remark, I began to think that maybe my tone had carried the intended suggestions—namely, that I was prison wise and potentially dangerous.

"Gotta earn their respect," I kept reminding myself, but that didn't lessen my fear. For the next fifteen years, I couldn't shake the feeling of being afraid to shower.

I had been assigned to F-Block, the prison segregation unit that was essentially one short step up from being in solitary confinement. It was also the cell block that housed Connecticut's death row and electric chair. I was confined to a small, one-man cell whose door was opened only for showers and an hour of recreation three times a week. During those rare trips outside the cell—even on the short walks to the shower room—I was required to wear shackles, lest there be any doubt about who was in control.

My small supply of commissary and toiletry items had been left behind at the county jail, so I had nothing except what the prison officials saw fit to give me. That included socks, two pairs of loose-fitting khakis, three changes of underwear and shirts, and a pair of stiff plastic sandals. I was also given a blanket and sheet to cover the thin, heavily stained mattress that lay on the narrow steel bunk in my cell. Permanently situated next to the bunk was a one-piece sink and toilet made entirely of stainless steel. The dirty-beige walls were emblazoned with graffiti that consisted almost exclusively of red-markered threats and curse words aimed at future Caucasian inmates, in this case me. Cell number eleven, F Block, was to be my home for more than six months.

During my stay there, I kept busy writing letters for my less literate peers. For my trouble I was sometimes rewarded with cigarettes or plastic containers of "pruno," as the prison-brewed wine was called. The quantities were occasionally sufficient to sustain my lingering lust for intoxication for a while. Heroin and cocaine were available through the cell-block tier man, a trustee who swept and mopped the halls, but the cost was high, and those who couldn't meet their drug debts were often beaten, sometimes turned out as prostitutes, or occasionally killed. That seemed a tremendous price to pay for a few hours of euphoria, so I got drunk whenever I could and stayed fairly comfortable with my stock of tobacco and rolling papers.

Being on continuous lockdown in the segregation unit allowed me a relatively safe perspective from which to view the world of prison. My preconceived notions about that world, based largely on old Humphrey Bogart and James Cagney movies, were of a place where it would be easy to tell the good guys from the bad. But I quickly realized that no such divisions were apparent. There were no good guys. There was just a sense of pervasive evil.

20. Transitional Unit

In the early fall of 1988, as I sat reviewing judicial documents for yet another segregation inmate who was looking for a loophole in his case, my cell was suddenly invaded by two corrections officers carrying green plastic trash bags. I thought I was about to be shaken down. Instead, I was told that prison officials had decided to move me to the transitional unit. I was not pleased.

Like the segregation unit, the Transitional Treatment Unit was a maximum-security housing area. It existed ostensibly for the purpose of helping new inmates make the adjustment to prison life. On the surface it sounded quite humanitarian, but that was hardly the case. Although it was classified as part of general-population housing, it actually functioned as the prison's psychiatric wing. Of the seventy or so inmates it housed, more than half were medicated with potent antipsychotic drugs, ranging from Thorazine and Mellaril to lithium and Depo Provera. A lesser proportion of them were either awaiting transfer to state psychiatric hospitals or being housed in this wing of the prison because they'd been removed from such hospitals, having proven themselves dangerous to those around them there. Several were serving life sentences for murder, rape, or assaults of a particularly savage nature. I was among the few who'd ended up in the unit because our attorneys had filed papers for a diminished-capacity defense, which apparently suggested to someone in the system that we needed *special attention*.

The evil I'd glimpsed in F-Block took on a much more ominous texture in TTU. Most of the men there spent their waking hours, often in filth and stench, watching small black-and-white portable televisions and talking back to them—mumbling at game-show hosts or cursing at the characters in movies and afternoon soap operas. After the tier lights were extinguished each night at nine o'clock, the cell block was bathed in an eerie glow from the TV sets, and my fellow inmates' mumbling turned to shrieks, disjointed chattering, and twisted, singsong ramblings. Soon after my transfer to that wing of the prison, I bought a small radio with a headset, and I listened to nothing but classical music over the local National Public Radio station. Bach, Beethoven, Mendelssohn, and Wagner became my aural guardians, effectively drowning out the vile cacophony generated by my fellow inmates and their idiot boxes.

Very late one night, well after midnight, I was lying awake, staring at the concrete-slab ceiling of my cell. Except for the heavy snoring that emanated from somewhere down the tier, the cell block was almost completely silent. It never annoyed me to find myself awake during such rare, quiet moments, because they allowed my mind to bathe in the peacefulness.

On that particular evening, though, my tranquil meditation

was abruptly disturbed by a gasping, gargling sound, like that of someone on the verge of retching. Sounding as if it came from the cell directly below mine, it continued for several minutes and was followed by a low, moaning noise. Then there was another gasp and the sound of the night guard's soft-soled shoes shuffling quickly down the tier. A moment later, the entire block was glaringly illuminated as the fluorescent main lights snapped on. The silence I'd been enjoying was immediately shattered by the angry shouts of rudely awakened inmates.

"Hey, stupid, turn off the fuckin' lights!"

"Yo, on the lights!"

Seconds later, the unmistakable sounds of jangling keys and heavy-booted footsteps heralded the arrival of a detachment of special emergency guards, otherwise known as the goon squad.

"Holy God in heaven!" cried one of them.

"Damn! Look at that! Call the hospital!" said another.

"Yeah, call the hospital. Now! I ain't touchin' this scumbag!" snapped a third guard.

"Hey, don't they look like little plums hanging there," said another member of the emergency unit.

"I gotta go be sick!" blurted out our night guard.

The next morning, we learned what had happened. One of the much-despised convicted rapists had tried to castrate himself with a razor. We didn't see him again for a long time after that incident. The most severe punishment, I concluded, is sometimes self-administered.

On another occasion, during the summer, one of the many seagulls that regularly soared and squawked around the prison got entangled in a coil of the razor wire that crowned the tall fences surrounding the facility. The anguished, almost human-sounding cries the bird made as it struggled to free itself echoed across the yard. This little tragedy happened to play itself out during recreation time, and a large group of inmates gathered at the windows of the cell-block recreation area to watch the scene. The more frantically the terrified gull fought to escape,

the more ensnared it became. Its feathers that had glimmered bright white against the sky turned to crimson and were torn from its body. One of its frail legs was severed. Meanwhile, the inmates at the window laughed and cursed the bird until the guards broke the crowd up and sent them back to their cells. The piercing cries of the gull continued. With each cry, even as they grew fainter, cheers went up from the caged men in TTU, until, finally, there was silence in the yard. Having been momentarily punctuated by a rare horror from without, life in the cell block resumed its cold, twisted regularity.

21. TURNING POINT

South Windsor, where I had lived during my attempt at self-rehabilitation, was about a half hour's drive south of the state prison, and the minister from the church I had attended there visited me at least once a month. Always rich with encouragement for the downtrodden, Pastor Bert Van Antwerpen would speak to me of God's faithfulness and forgiveness, and he would share humorous asides concerning his family or members of his congregation. Seated across the table from me in the visiting room, he would also pray for me. I appreciated his visits, but I was still so filled with anger, fear, and shame that I was generally unresponsive to his message. That changed after I told him about an incident in the cell block involving two of the other inmates.

Lester, the tierman in TTU, was an industrious fellow, tall, in good physical condition, and devoutly religious. He swept the floors with one hand on a broom or a mop and the other on his Bible. He often fasted and sometimes went for days without talking to anyone. When he was in speaking mode, he talked about learning to temper and control his lusts. That kind of discussion might have struck me as odd if I'd heard it anywhere other than in TTU, but in that environment it struck me as relatively normal. Lester also liked to talk about his Bible studies and his faith in Jesus, although few inmates in the cell block were willing to listen. I never felt particularly close to him, but I talked with him almost daily as he swept and mopped the floor in front of my cell.

On that particular afternoon, he was going about his usual routine, sharing his words of faith and thoughts of the day as he slowly made his way along the tier. Suddenly, from a cell several doors down, an inmate named Jerry Bender began to shout angrily. A fat man in his thirties, Bender had a habit of regularly inciting the "crazies" in TTU to start screaming matches. After he got them going, he would sit back and laugh, feeding the wild bantering when it started to ebb. I hated Bender and considered him especially dangerous, although I had no idea what crime he had been convicted of. That afternoon, his attention focused on Lester, at whom he began screaming and throwing things from his cell.

"Get away from my damn house, you moron!" raged Bender.

"You're messing up the floor, my man," Lester lightly countered.

"I don't give a damn about the floor!" Bender shot back at him. "And I sure don't give a damn about you or your fuckin'

Jesus neither! You hear me, Lester? I don't give a damn about you or Jesus. Hey, idiot, you know something? You wanna know something? If I'd been there when they stuck his ass up on that cross, I would've laughed! I would've been right there hollering at him to come down!"

Then, in typical fashion, Bender started to call out a cadence: "What we gonna do to Jesus? Crucify! Crucify! What we gonna do to Jesus? Crucify! Crucify!"

Soon the block reverberated with the chant, accompanied by frenzied clamoring. Men banged shoes on footlockers; rolls of flaming toilet paper came streaming out of several cells; and all manner of garbage began collecting on the tier. Through it all, the contemptuous laughter of Jerry Bender roared in the background. After initially seeming to be entertained by the display of psychotic irreverence, a guard finally called the goon squad to restore a semblance of order to the cell block. But after the goons did their work, the entire scene left something deep inside me feeling sick, angry, and sad for a long time.

When I next saw Lester, I couldn't help but notice that he wasn't carrying his Bible.

"Where's the Good Book," I asked him.

"Got to give it a break, my man," he replied. "Just got to give it a break."

The following week, I recounted the whole episode to Pastor Bert and told him how it had made me feel. Expecting him to be shocked by the story, I figured he would assure me of Bender's certain damnation. But he was neither shocked nor accusatory. Instead, a quiet sadness came over his face as he reached across the tabletop and took my hands in his. Tears welled up in his eyes, and he fixed a gentle, childlike gaze on me. When he finally spoke, he softly stammered a question: "Do you think, Ray, that if you and I were standing in the crowd at the foot of the cross, we would have behaved any differently?"

Silence.

I wanted to answer "Yes," but I couldn't. And in that moment I was overcome with a sense that the most obvious thing in the world had been pointed out to me. I realized that I was not and had never been some brave soldier of the Lord. At the same time, I understood Bert's sadness, beneath which I sensed a broader sorrow—the kind of soul sadness a father might feel at watching his children destroy their lives. I went back to my cell and cried.

At first I wasn't sure why I was crying, but my feeling was one of profound grief, and my mind was filled with images and thoughts I hadn't revisited in many years. I thought of Christ crucified, condemned to death because he'd encouraged others to love and care for one another. I thought of the jeers and humiliation he must have known. I thought of the pitiful men, my peers, who'd laughed and cheered at the agony of a trapped and dying seagull. A veil, it seemed, had been lifted from my eyes and I suddenly understood that all things are interconnected. I thought of the hopes, plans, and dreams of my family. I recalled the ideals I had once cherished. My mind was flooded with visions of the past. I considered not the predictability of the church services I had faithfully attended as a child but the strength I drew from being part of them. I remembered my heroes—Mickey Mantle, Whitey Ford, President Kennedy, the astronauts of the early NASA space program, and Father Griffin, a young priest at Holy Family Church whose strong anti-segregationist stance had moved him to march on Washington with Martin Luther King Jr. These were the people who had inspired my youth.

I thought of my mother and the pain she must have felt at seeing her only son sent to prison. I remembered my father and considered the beautiful, gentle man he was at heart. Like me, he had wanted to be a perfect dad but was tragically hindered by alcoholism, a grossly misunderstood disease. For the first time in my life, I felt pity and forgiveness toward him. I sobbed deeply.

Prayers came next. I asked God to come back into my life, and I haltingly muttered Latin phrases that I hadn't spoken since my childhood—"Kyrie eleison, kyrie eleison; Lord have mercy, Lord have mercy." I said the Act of Contrition and asked Christ to forgive me for my sins. I prayed and petitioned the Almighty almost incessantly over the next several days. The faith I had known as a boy assured me that my prayers were heard and would be acted upon. I prayed that I would be kept safe. I asked God to somehow open the doors of the prison for me—to send angels to protect me and lead me from captivity. Jesus had said, "Knock at the door, and it shall be opened unto you." So I knocked with a fervor that I felt was surely keeping the angels up at night. I expected nothing less than a miracle.

22. Holiday Project

It was the Christmas season of 1988, and several weeks had passed since my epiphany and repentance. So far, no choir of angels had shown up to escort me out of prison, nor had I received word that the governor had reviewed my case and decided I deserved a second chance. It was simply business as usual at TTU, with the crazies, Jerry Bender, and Lester, who I was happy to see was once again carrying his Bible.

The small black-and-white television that I had in my cell, courtesy of the prison TV-loaner program, was sad company. The endless series of commercials advertising upcoming Christmas specials and televised holiday parades only served to remind me of all the places I would rather have been than in the slammer. College football bowl games were also being heavily advertised, and I couldn't help but notice that Michigan was slated to play Southern California in the annual Rose Bowl game. It occurred to me that Pasadena would be a nice place to be come January first.

As I reminisced about the good times I'd known during my college-era trips to Ann Arbor, Jerry Bender blubbered up to my cell, having been let out of his to help Lester with custodial duties. "Yo, knucklehead," he greeted me. "You interested in puttin' any bets on the bowl games? Pack a cigarettes, bar a soap? You could be a big winner!"

"Nah," I said, holding on to the cold bars of my cell. "I don't think so."

"Yeah, well listen," he continued. "I'm gonna have some brew ready for Christmas, too. Don't tell any of these other jerk-offs. I figure you're cool. Two packs of smokes for a quart. It'll really get you in the spirit, if you know what I mean."

I blew off Bender's second offer as well—"Not this time, Jerry." My refusal wasn't only motivated by the fact that I didn't trust him but also by my realization that I wasn't interested in getting drunk. He started to walk away, mumbling curses under his breath, and I was just about to return to my bunk when I noticed a pair of socks hanging on the tier railing about two cells down. They were new-looking white tube socks with dark blue and yellow stripes—maize and blue.

"Yo, Jerry!" I called out.

He turned around and walked back to my cell. "Change your mind?" he asked with a grin.

"No," I said, "but I wonder if you know whose socks those are with the blue and yellow stripes?"

"You need socks? Hey, I can get you socks! My *boy* works in the prison clothing room. Three pair for a pack—new."

Typical of Bender, I thought—trying to get away with selling something that inmates could get for free with a simple request order.

"No, I want those," I emphatically told him.

Muttering barely audible curses again, he walked over to the neighboring cell and began talking with the owner of the maize-and-blue-striped socks. "Yo," he said, looking back at me, "he says you can have 'em for a pack a cigarettes."

It was a steep price to pay for a pair of socks, but I wanted them. So I took a pack of smokes from my footlocker and tossed them to the fat middleman. He immediately opened it and removed two cigarettes—his commission for cutting the deal, I figured—then came back with my purchase.

"Here." He handed the socks to me. "You need anything else, you let me know."

"Yeah, thanks," I told him as he waddled away.

Standing there with my newly acquired socks and thoughts of trips to a spectacularly crowded Michigan Stadium, I longed to be in Cerebral City again, shoulder to shoulder with old friends in the stands as we cheered for the Wolverines. The richly colored stripes on the socks had a sheen to them that reminded me of the jerseys and embroidered hats that were ubiquitous in Ann Arbor. Suddenly I could almost hear David Hunsberger, as if he were standing right beside me, yelling about Woodstock and joining me in the familiar chant "Let's go, Blue!"

It was a fond but hopeless nostalgic thought, I realized. Still, it filled me with happiness, and as I turned around, still lost in my daydream, my attention was inexplicably drawn to a plastic Rubbermaid bowl that I used for storing coffee. Another inmate had given it to me when he was released. Because the lid wasn't on it, I noticed that the bowl's circular mouth was roughly the size of the sewing hoop my grandmother used when she was doing embroidery. That comparison unleashed a flood of images from yet another period of my past. Grandma Hattie had died in 1976, after several years of mental deterioration, but in my mind's eye I could see her in her rocker on the porch of the house on York Road, where she would spend hours at her craft. Oblivious to the world, she seemed to enjoy a reflective peace as she stitched, and she would always smile up at me when I happened to find her so engaged.

That's when I made a decision: In my own way, I was going to Pasadena to attend the Rose Bowl and cheer the Wolverines on to victory. I was as excited as if a taxi were about to whisk me away from the prison and deliver me to Bradley International Airport for a flight to southern California.

In that exultant state of mind, I emptied the remains of my coffee container into a paper cup, then rinsed out the bowl and went to work cutting off its circular mouth. With the limited tools I had on hand—a spool of heavy-duty thread and the same kind of nail clippers I had earlier used to craft objects essential to my short-lived jailbreak—it proved to be a laborious task. I dismantled the clippers and used one of the blades to etch a groove all the way around the bowl, about an inch below the top. During the procedure, a corrections officer on his way past my cell paused to watch my activities and looked bemused. Having completed the surface cut, I stretched about a ten-inch length of the thread between my hands, lined it up in the groove I'd made, and started moving it back and forth so that it sawed into the plastic. The thread frayed quickly and broke often from the force of the friction, but I just kept pulling more of it off the spool. In that fashion, it took me the better part of an afternoon to cut the mouth from the bowl, transforming it into a sewing hoop that would've made Grandma Hattie proud. Using the same process, I cut another ring from the bowl's snap-on lid to use as a fitted loop that would hold a piece of cloth tightly in place.

Next, I drew a simple block-letter M on a torn-off scrap from the sheet on my bunk. After securing my design cloth onto the hoop, I set about pulling the thread from my maize-and-blue-striped socks—a task that, at first, proved to be trickier than I had anticipated. But after I discovered that socks are made so that they can easily unravel from the toe up, my work proceeded much more smoothly. As I gradually removed the bright nylon thread and wound it around the barrel of a pen, I was pleasantly surprised by the substantial amount of it that could be gleaned from a single tube-sock stripe.

It occurred to me that I could complete my sewing kit in purist fashion by waiting for fish to be served in the prison mess hall, pulling a bone from one of the "fillets," and using it to fashion a needle. But it proved much more efficient to ask a guard's permission to sign one out. Sewing needles were made available to inmates for the purposes of mending or replacing buttons on shirts and pants. As long as the cell-block officer was in a cooperative mood, they could be signed out routinely. Perhaps because the Christmas season lent itself to a spirit of magnanimity, I was able to easily acquire a needle in time to begin my project the following day.

I erroneously presumed that if little old ladies could embroider fancy designs onto tablecloths and pillowcases, as my Grandma Hattie had, the task would be easy for me as well. It was not. An hour into the project, I stopped counting the number of times I pricked my fingers. In the meantime, I had to interrupt my work frequently to untangle knots in the sock thread. It was a tedious learning process, but I persevered. I worked on my Michigan M for two days, during which I learned a great deal about handling a needle and experienced a deep sense of enjoyment in the process. I also felt something I hadn't felt in a long time—pride in myself. I was quite pleased with the results of my efforts. I had constructed something with my own hands that made me feel genuinely good about myself, and I wanted to prolong the feeling.

I needed a hat, so, with blue shoelaces, scraps of cloth I collected from other inmates, and the elastic waistband from a pair of boxer shorts, I pieced and sewed together a simple visor cap. In keeping with my maize-and-blue theme, I used a yellow Hi-Liter pen to "dye" the elastic. The next step—cutting the M from my base cloth and attaching it to the cap's bill—concerned me, because it required a sharp tool. It was easy to dismantle a disposable razor and remove the blade, but I knew that if I were discovered with a loose razor blade in my possession, I could be in serious trouble. A homemade weapon with just such a blade had recently been used in an attack on a Somers corrections officer, and the prison was on high alert for the possibility of any further violence of that kind. For that reason, I was extremely cautious about cutting out my embroidered handiwork, and after the razor blade had served its purpose, I flushed it down the toilet.

With the M in place, my cap was completed, and I sat back to admire my creation. It wasn't really a thing of beauty, but it was my own in a way that felt magical. It was the key ingredient in an otherwise simple plan, the next step of which called for the purchase of a large bag of cheese popcorn and a canister of iced tea from the prison commissary. Come January first, I was going to be watching the Rose Bowl and cheering Michigan on to glorious victory. I was confident that my hat would successfully transport my spirit, if not my body, to Pasadena. I was happy. I had a dream!

23. Piecework on Commission

During an otherwise gloomy Christmas week in the TTU, many of the inmates were treated to a welcome deviation from the cell block's routine circumstances and diet. This was thanks to the prison's package program, which allowed us to receive modest, carefully inspected gifts of food and clothing. A number of men began skipping scheduled meals and wearing colorful sweatshirts. New baseball caps also appeared on a number of inmates' heads, but none of them attracted more attention than the "magical Michigan cap" that I had begun wearing regularly.

Because the package program's regulations prohibited monograms or product logos on clothing we received, everyone wanted to know how I had managed to get an embroidered hat into the prison. A mystique immediately surrounded my handcrafted maize-and-blue headgear, which—I was proud to discover—my fellow inmates presumed to be store-bought. I was even more flattered when requests for embroidery work started coming in.

As I sat on my bunk one afternoon, a Latino inmate from another cell block suddenly appeared at my door. Introducing himself as Miguel, he said he'd heard about my hat from another inmate. He wanted to see it for himself.

"Listen," he said after inspecting the cap, "do you think you could make a Puerto Rican flag about the size of that M?"

"Well," I hedged, "I'm not sure."

"I pay you. I pay you good up front," he said.

"Sounds good," I replied, caught off guard by the offer. "But I've only got blue and yellow thread."

"You need red, white, and blue," said Miguel. "I can get you some colored socks. I bring them by tomorrow, with a down payment. I want five flags. I'll give you five cartons of cigarettes. Newports okay?"

I was flabbergasted. Five cartons of cigarettes was a lot of "money" in prison terms. The offer seemed a little too good to be true, but I told Miguel that I'd get started just as soon as I had the socks he had promised. We shook hands, and he scurried out of TTU, glancing into a few of the cells as he left, apparently stunned by the disgustingly unclean conditions in which some of the block's inmates chose to live.

I didn't expect him to come back, and when I didn't see him the next day, I wrote him off and all but forgot about the deal we had struck. It was just as well that he hadn't returned, I figured, because it occurred to me that I could end up doing a lot of work and not get paid. Then I'd be marked as a chump and might be forced into doing free embroidery for all the gang members in the prison.

Two days later, my discussion with Miguel about the embroidered flags was far from my mind as I tuned in the Rose Bowl game on my loaner portable TV and quickly became immersed in the action. Michigan was playing well and looked to be the sure winner. My homemade cap felt great on my head as I sipped iced tea, chomped on stale popcorn, and chanted, "Go Blue!" with the fans, as though I were sitting in the stands with them. All things considered, I was having an exceptional time.

"Yo, Sock Man," came a half-whispered call to me through the cell bars. It was Miguel. "Hey, sorry I didn't make it over yesterday. The C.O. wouldn't let me in the block. Here's what I said." He pushed a brown paper bag through the bars.

Taking the bag, I looked inside to find several pairs of new tube socks with a variety of colored stripes at the tops, as well as two cartons of cigarettes. "Cool," I said with a smile.

"You said Newports would be all right!" Miguel shot back, obviously thinking I was suddenly changing my terms, demanding another brand of menthols.

"No, I mean, fine. Good. I'll get going on the project right away," I said.

"Take your time, man. Do a good job. I'll stop back next week," he replied before leaving the cell block.

I felt rich. Two cartons of cigarettes and five pairs of new socks with the labels still on them! Making the little flags, I knew, would keep me busy for a while. I said a silent prayer of thanks and hopped back onto my bunk just as Michigan scored another touchdown.

"Go, Blue!" I shouted as I wondered how many stripes were on the Puerto Rican flag.

It took me about three and a half weeks to complete all five of the flags, each measuring two and a half by three inches. I was pleased with the way they looked, and so was everyone I showed them to, including, most importantly, Miguel. He had paid me the remaining three cartons after seeing the first completed flag, and he'd also brought me two more pairs of socks. It was only later that I came to appreciate what a phenomenal marketing opportunity the flag commission turned out to be.

Over the next several months, I was inundated with requests for embroidered mini-flags—not only Puerto Rican but also Italian and Confederate flags, and one Korean flag. In addition,

I turned out logos of various sports teams. Honoring on my first commission, I charged a carton of cigarettes for a flag and half a carton for single- or double-letter monograms. Business was thriving. Everybody paid on time, and I never heard even the slightest complaint regarding my workmanship. If I needed a particular color of thread to complete a commission, I would let it be known, and as if by magic, a pair of socks with the thread color I needed would show up in my cell the next day.

With head bowed over my sewing hoop, I began talking to God as I worked. I thanked him for giving me something to do to fill my time and earn an income. Having no cigarettes in the joint—being "caught out," as the expression went—was the worst of all possible worlds. The needlework also afforded time for soul-searching, and I began taking stock of my faults and defeats as well as the victories I'd achieved in my life. Waking up in prison every morning tended to reinforce a low self-opinion, regardless of any previous triumphs. So I thrived on the positive feedback I received from both my fellow inmates and the corrections officers who became familiar with my sewing activities. A few of these officers even commissioned work from me.

I became familiar with the policy that forbade needlework one afternoon when I approached a supervising captain who was touring the cell block. A fellow inmate had suggested that I might want to display examples of my work in the small inmate art showcase that was on a wall in the visitors' waiting room. It sounded like a good idea, so I approached Captain Galewhite in order to show him my latest creation, a rather complex hearts-

and-flowers design with the words "I Love You, Mom" sewn into it.

"Sir, Captain Galewhite," I called out as I approached him from behind.

"What is it?" he asked, turning to look at me.

"Well, sir, I do this artwork," I said. I lifted my sewing hoop to show him my work. "And—"

"That's embroidery, Materson," he interrupted, giving the piece only a passing glance. "That's contraband."

"I was wondering if I could display it, sir. Everybody thinks—"

Before I could say anything else, the captain turned on his heel, shaking his head. "I didn't even see that, Materson. Embroidery. Contraband."

It was never quite clear to me why something as innocuous as embroidery could be considered contraband. I figured that maybe the regulations banning inmates from "altering provisions or objects from their original, intended purpose or use" must have been the technicality that made my activities illicit. But that rule seemed to have been designed to address the popular inmate practice of making shanks out of everything from mop handles to toothbrushes—not to mention situations such as my own fabrication of a fake gun from ordinary commissary items. Still, a needlework image that said, "I Love You, Mom" seemed a far cry from a crudely fashioned knife or a phony pistol. But I wasn't about to make an issue out of the rule—not at the risk of losing my creative outlet. Captain Galewhite had said he didn't see it, so I left well enough alone.

If there was a downside to being the cell-block embroiderer, it was in terms of my image among my fellow prisoners, more than a few of whom began speculating about my sexual orientation. One inmate, who vaguely resembled my junior-high-school nemesis, Charlie Larsen, delighted in referring to me as "Betsy Ross."

Long before I took up embroidery, I had come to realize that prison was a world controlled by the law of primitive survival. In many ways, it was like being plunged back into adolescence. It was seventh-grade bullies all over again. But the bullies in this world were bigger, more numerous, and far meaner, and they generally lacked a very basic ingredient for growth: hope.

Sustained by a renewed faith, I had found hope again. I had forgiveness in my heart, and the embroidery provided the mental focus I needed. Still, not a day passed when I wasn't instinctively on guard and even frightened by most of the people I saw every day. I avoided confrontation whenever possible, because I had seen the most trivial arguments between inmates erupt into bloody brawls that brought swift, harsh punishment from the authorities. I had no desire to be maimed or killed in prison; nor did I want to be sent to the hole. And I certainly didn't want to parlay my already formidable sentence into an even longer term, as I'd seen other inmates do by participating in fights that brought about injuries and further court cases.

Standing in line for lunch one day, I found myself between two arguing gang members. Whatever the fundamental subject at issue might have been, it was quickly lost as the tension and anger escalated. Taunts between the two men soon turned into threats of violence, and one of them pushed me aside to get in the other's face. The next thing I knew, a fist was thrown. Like ripples on a dismal pond, the ugly energy in the surrounding space began to spread out. I don't want to be in the middle of this, I thought to myself. Then, quite out of nowhere, Miguel—the Puerto Rican guy who gave me my first embroidery commission—stepped right into the center of the escalating violence. Spouting a few commands in Spanish, he grabbed one of the brawling men by the collar.

"Yo, this man here"—he pointed directly at me—"he did work for me." As the combatants directed their attention toward me, Miguel explained in a threatening tone, "I don't want anything to happen to this guy. *Comprende*?"

The fight was over as quickly as it had begun. I breathed a sigh of relief and whispered a prayer of thanksgiving. Embroidery had some far-reaching benefits, I mused to myself as I returned to my place in the chow line.

24. A Calling Rewarded

In the fall and into the early winter of 1989, the embroidery commissions from my fellow inmates tended to become increasingly intricate with each request. I practiced my drawing and design techniques—a process that didn't come easily, because I'd had no previous experience studying art or making artwork. I had, however, visited a few art museums during my childhood and my college years. In those days I had been especially drawn to the paintings of Claude Monet and the other French Impressionists, although I wasn't exactly sure why.

I was on my bunk stitching one afternoon when an elderly inmate shuffled up to my cell. I recognized him, having seen him almost daily since my arrival at TTU, but I'd never spoken with him and didn't know his name. He was pale and slightly hunchbacked, wore horn-rimmed glasses, and looked perpetually in need of a shave.

"I'm leaving today," he mumbled. "Being released to a halfway house."

"Hey, that's good, Pops," I said.

'Well, anyway," he continued, "I'm giving some things away that I've collected over the years. I thought you might find some use for this."

Through the bars he handed me a book—*Impressionism,* by Phoebe Pool. I accepted the gift and thanked the old-timer. He wished me well and told me to stay out of trouble; then he was gone.

I continually reflected on how I had happened to begin embroidering, and on the fact that it kept me well supplied with cigarettes, the universal prison currency. I repeatedly recalled the near fight in the cafeteria, from which I had been rescued by a satisfied customer. Being an embroidery artist in the midst of the coarse, violent, macho world of prison seemed absurd, but I came to firmly believe that this was my true vocation, my calling.

So when an old stranger passed me a book that furthered my prior interest in French Impressionism, the natural thing for me to do was to follow the lead. To test my hunch that my sock-thread embroidery might lend itself to an Impressionist style, I made postage-stamp-sized sketches of three pieces of art reproduced in the book. Then, with great patience, I embroidered reproductions of the works. They pleased me so much that I sewed them onto a headband and mailed it to my daughter, Sue.

Between commissions for sports-team and Harley-Davidson logos, I continued to experiment with imagery and design. I felt I should create pieces in a uniform size, but I wasn't sure what size. I put the question to Jason Mobry, a fellow inmate who had been a photographer prior to the murder for which he'd received a life term. He minced no words: "If these images of yours were ever photographed," he said, "two and a quarter by two and three-quarter inches would be ideal." So that's the format I chose.

When Jason married his college sweetheart, with whom he'd corresponded for many years from prison, I designed an image based on Shakespeare's *A Midsummer Night's Dream* and gave it to him as a wedding present. He was delighted with it, and he continued to be a good source of creative advice.

Embroidering the Shakespearean image for Jason reopened my mind and heart to my first artistic love—theater—and I began thinking about scenes from other plays that I might interpret in needlework. Hamlet was an obvious choice for me, because his tragedy of irresolution had been the theme of a paper I wrote in college. I replayed the drama in my mind and made small drawings of scenes from each of its five acts, then transformed them into embroidered images. As I worked, I was approached daily by curious inmates.

"Yo, my man, what you making there?" Lester inquired one morning.

"It's a scene from a play called *Hamlet,*" I explained, climbing off my bunk and stepping over to the cell bars. The scene I was working on depicted Prince Hamlet walking along a castle parapet, his sword upraised in one hand as he pursued his father's ghost. I explained it to Lester, giving him a brief synopsis of the play.

"So this man's uncle killed his pops and then married his mom?" Lester asked.

"Yes," I told him. "That's where it all began."

"Damn, if it ain't like Cain and Abel all over again," he spouted with great enthusiasm.

"Exactly," I responded. "But the play has more to do with Hamlet's uncertainty as to what he should do about it. See, he's pretty sure that he knows the deal about the murder. He knows he should take revenge if it's the truth. But he keeps having these little doubts. He even thinks that maybe he should kill himself."

"Well," Lester concluded, "if he knew more about the Bible, he would know that the Lord avenges. Hamlet here got no faith. See, if you follow the Lord, no matter what kind of misery you find yourself in, he'll get ya through it. The man should've prayed more and thought less."

Having completed the series of Hamlet scenes just prior to Christmas 1989, I began work on a group of images from the Bible. For me, it was a way of celebrating and giving thanks for the new life I'd found in faith and artwork. As it turned out, working on that series helped propel me into a new dimension of creative expression. By framing the biblical scenes against the rich backdrops of images from the Impressionism book, I discovered the importance of shadow and depth. My work on the scriptural series blossomed into a deep, spiritual experience in which I immersed myself. The gratitude in my heart nurtured a spirit of forgiveness that enabled me, finally, to look back on my life without shame. Living outside the shadow of shame became a theme for my life as well as my art. A window had been opened in my life.

Another window opened for me only a few weeks after I completed the series of biblical scenes. Jason Mobry strode up to my cell one day and showed me a folk art magazine. "You should think about contacting these people," he said, pointing to an advertisement. "You could probably make some real money if you sold your work out in the real world."

The magazine ad announced sites for a traveling craft and folk art show. The sponsoring organization was listed as Country Folk Art Shows, Inc., and the address indicated that it happened to be headquartered on the outskirts of Ann Arbor, Michigan—Cerebral City, home of the Wolverines, for me the site of so many fond, if somewhat hazy, memories of college escapades.

I promptly composed a letter to the organizers of the folk art show, explaining my circumstances and describing the kind of work I was making. I told them I would very much like to exhibit my art with them, if arrangements could be made for that to happen. It felt like the right thing to do, and I was infused with a spirit of optimism as I sent the letter off.

Within a week I was rewarded with a letter from Country Folk Art Shows, Inc. I could see the return-address logo on the envelope as the block officer passed it through the bars of my cell. The letter expressed interest in my work and requested photographs of some of the pieces. Of course, I was thrilled to have gotten a response in such a short time, but I had no photos to send. So, in my wholly optimistic state of mind, I wrote another letter and enclosed an actual piece of my work in the envelope. I didn't give a thought to the possibility that it might be lost or stolen and I might hear nothing else from the people at Country Folk Art Shows. I was operating on pure faith.

Considering how many hands mail has to pass through in the prison system, it was no small miracle that I received a response to my second letter only five days after I sent it. The letter from Michigan was full of glowing praise for my work, and it was accompanied by a consignment contract. I was ecstatic. Scanning the enclosed list of sites for upcoming shows, I noticed that the Polo Grounds in Farmington, Connecticut, was scheduled to host one in mid-June. I appreciated the irony of presenting an incarcerated bottom-dweller's artwork before the kind of socially elite crowd that would no doubt dominate the audience at that venue, so I decided that Farmington was where my art would make its public debut.

My next task was to find someone who was willing and able to take my work to the show. I decided to ask my sister, Barbara, if she could do me the favor. After a few personal struggles of her own, she had settled her life and was raising twin daughters as a single parent in Albany, New York. Her time was precious, but she told me in a letter that she would be happy to take my artwork to Connecticut. She said she was delighted that I was doing something positive with my time, having read and heard horrific reports about life behind bars. She constantly worried about me, she said.

As the winter months gave way to spring, I concentrated on making new pieces for the Polo Grounds exhibit. I created images based on theatrical dramas, song lyrics, and personal experience, and each one, in its own way, celebrated feelings, dreams, or self-examination. I worked from the time the lights went on in the cell block in the morning to the time they were dimmed in the evening. I laughed as I considered that I was perhaps the only inmate to ever complain that there wasn't enough time in a day.

By the time June rolled around, I had seventeen pieces ready for the show. Accompanying each one with a brief written explanation of its significance, I double-wrapped them in paper and sent them to Barbara in Albany.

• • •

25. "I Think I Made You Up Inside My Head"

Having completed what I thought of as a respectable body of work for the Polo Grounds exhibit, I didn't slow down or take a break. I continued to work and to experiment, always led by my feelings.

Often those feelings were evoked by music—by the drama in Dvořák's and Wagner's powerful orchestral works, for example, or by a handful of tapes I'd purchased through the prison "Music Club," notably Joni Mitchell's *For the Roses*. Ever since my college days, I had admired her songs of deep love, broken hearts, and lost dreams. It was dreary stuff to listen to in prison, but it reminded me that I had loved and had felt joy, sorrow, and tenderness, and it made me yearn to experience those feelings again.

With Joni Mitchell singing in the background, I reread *The Bell Jar,* by Sylvia Plath, and felt myself profoundly touched by her evocation of her confused, troubled life. In my initial, college-lit-class reading of the book, I had somehow missed Plath's short villanelle "Mad Girl's Love Song," printed at the end of the book, but now I found it so powerful that I memorized it.

> I fancied you'd return the way you said,
> But I grow old and I forget your name.
> (I think I made you up inside my head.)

I could readily relate to the notion of making up the perfect love inside my own head, and, although I had no particular woman in mind, I began praying to God for her appearance. To attract the love of a woman while in prison seemed like the remotest of fantasies, but somehow, I felt that the time was right.

THE AFTERNOON'S COUNT HAD JUST been completed on Monday, September 10, 1990, and Corrections Officer Manning was walking slowly along the cell-block tier passing out mail. I was on my bunk sewing a new piece that I'd titled *Girl in the Mirror*. I had recently become fascinated with the concept of reflection, and I was struck by the fact that the depiction of a reflected image could add a sense of depth and a mysterious inquiry to an artistic rendering.

"Materson, mail," called Manning through the cell bars.

He handed me a small lavender envelope. The handwriting on it looked feminine, and the return address was an unfamiliar one in Albany. As I took it in my hand, I swear, I felt a curious spark of energy flow up my arm from my fingertips.

"Girlfriend?" the guard wondered teasingly.

"It's possible, Mr. Manning. It's possible."

The letter was from a woman named Melanie Hohman, who had seen the work I'd sent to the Polo Grounds show and been "floored by it," she wrote. Through cinder-block walls, over coils of razor wire, and across many miles, I had touched her. More importantly, she now touched me—with her honesty, and with her description of her own personal problems. I read her letter repeatedly, sometimes tracing her handwriting with my fingertip. The moment reminded me of all the possibilities still out there in the world.

Immediately, I pulled a notepad from under my mattress.

But as I sat poised to write, I found myself unsure of how to phrase my reply. Feeling the urge to explode onto the page with Byronesque verse was wonderful, but my more contained, practical side suggested a more tempered response—interested but not overly enthusiastic. Instead of choosing one approach over the other, I attempted to strike a sort of balance between them. It took me a few hours to compose the letter, in which I told her I was flattered by her comments about my art and responded to a few other particulars she had mentioned. When I was satisfied with the letter, I carefully folded it and slipped it into an envelope that I then addressed and dropped into the inmate mailbox on my way to the evening meal. No sooner had I done so than the worry set in. Had I said too much? Had I not said enough? Was my tone too aloof?

To distract myself from such thoughts, I reimmersed myself in my work on *Girl in the Mirror.* Asleep later that night, I dreamed about the woman I'd never met.

THE NEXT DAY, AS I STRODE back to my cell from lunch in the prison cafeteria, I was still thinking of Melanie and considering the prospect of writing her another letter. Suddenly there was a commotion in the corridor; red lights flashed and emergency buzzers sounded. Guards began running past me, some of them pulling on riot gear as they rushed toward the cafeteria that I had left only moments before. Other guards approached inmates and hurried us to our respective cell blocks. Tense voices could be heard over crackling walkie-talkies as they called for backup: "All available officers. Code red in the main cafeteria. Repeat: Code red."

As I moved quickly toward my block, I saw Officer Manning pulling inmates through the door. "Take it in! Lock it up!" he shouted repeatedly. A few inmates were hesitating, looking back in the direction of the trouble. A couple of gang members came tearing down the hallway, pushing their way past other inmates, apparently intent on participating in whatever was going on in the cafeteria. I felt comforted when Officer Manning grabbed my shoulder and pushed me into the cell block, and I wasted no time in getting back to my cage. The block echoed with whoops and screamed obscenities. I climbed up on my bunk, still pondering a woman named Melanie.

A trio of guards walked through the block, banging on cell doors and making sure all of them were locked. They pointedly ignored the barrage of shouted questions and demands from inmates who wanted to know what was happening. We didn't find out until later that evening, when the local TV news reported that three guards at Somers prison had been jumped during the noon meal. One had been stabbed in the throat and was in serious condition at Hartford Hospital. Pictures of the other two showed their faces covered with cuts and bruises. Several inmates had also been injured in the melee, which was reported to have been gang-related. As a result of all this, the prison had been placed on lockdown status. Cheers went up from other cells every time the faces of the injured guards were shown during the newscast. I was sickened as I thought of the guards and the terror they must have felt during the assault.

The lockdown lasted for almost a week. During the first few days, we were fed bag lunches in our cells and not even permitted to take showers. Then there were the inevitable shakedowns, with teams of guards methodically inspecting cells, sifting through inmates' belongings, and searching for weapons, drugs, or anything that even remotely resembled contraband. My cell was no exception. My books, clothes, toiletry items, and snack foods were thrown about, and my bunk was stripped. Socks and spools of thread that I'd collected over the previous year were tossed carelessly into a large garbage bag, and—worst of all—a plastic mug that still had some grape Kool-Aid in it was dumped into the bag with them.

It took about ten minutes for the guards to ransack my cell. They asked about the dozens of Bic pen barrels that I used as spools for the unraveled sock thread, and I patiently explained their presence and the purpose for which I used them. The guards didn't seem interested.

I had been through shakedowns before, but none had left me feeling so violated as this one did. My livelihood had been seriously disrupted. My cell looked as though it has been hit by a tornado, and I suddenly found it easy to imagine how survivors of severe storms feel. Although the chaos in my cell was of minor significance compared to a devastated house, the empty pain that it made me feel was as real as that of anyone who has had their home destroyed. My cell was my entire world. Slowly, patiently, I began putting everything back in order.

26. MELANIE

Melanie's life had seen its share of stormy circumstances, I found out within the first month of our correspondence. She'd been abused as a child and abandoned by her natural father, and she had seen her mother die as a result of careless medical treatment of her intestinal cancer. Melanie had planned on an art career, but her portfolio had been stolen within her first few weeks as a freshman at the University of Texas. Lacking the self-confidence that might have helped her overcome that setback, she'd hit the road, in part to seek ad-

venture and come to terms with her own identity, but also to escape the pain of her childhood and youth.

Redirecting her creative energies toward singing and songwriting, Melanie traveled the country attending concerts. Her favorite performers were Bob Dylan, Patti Smith, and John Cale, and she also had a particular fondness for gospel choirs. Alcohol and drugs fit an image she had chosen for herself at the time and also served to ease the unhappiness. She moved to New York's Greenwich Village, seemingly an ideal place to be an iconoclastic musician in the 1970s—partying with the New York Dolls and the crowd at CBGB, the city's premier punk-rock showcase—and she even took on the role of lead singer in a punk band.

Melanie's letters were like songs to me. In them, she sang of happy, rebellious times when she sported blue-streaked hair and wore men's satin pajamas on the streets of lower Manhattan. She sang of her experiments incorporating the sounds of breaking glass, pounding trash cans, and the doleful hum of appliance motors into her music. And she cried a woeful ballad about her friends and fellow musicians who had died from drug overdoses. It was these repeated contacts with death, complicated by her own growing addiction, that prompted her retreat from the city.

After leaving New York, Melanie continued to experiment with writing. She wrote about the agony of her incidents of drunkenness, and of her abusive relationships. And she wrote about birds, which she saw as heralds, harbingers, and friends. As I read her letters, I paid closer attention to the cries of the gulls that relentlessly circled about the prison towers. In my mind, those were her cries.

I fell in love.

"YOU NEED TO FIND AN AGENT," she had told me in one of her first letters. That simple advice struck me as brilliant, exciting, flattering, and, at the same time, ludicrous. In my mind, my circumstances made the notion of finding a qualified professional to represent my art to the world seem impossible. I wrote back to Melanie with thanks for the suggestion and a suggestion of my own: "Why don't you be my agent?"

"I'm just a waitress," she responded in her next letter. As I read those words, I thought back on my own sense of inadequacy when I was "just a busboy," and I felt even closer to her. Life had left her, too, feeling shortchanged and frustrated.

"I'm just a prison inmate," I wrote back to her. "I'm the lowest rung on the social ladder. You, on the other hand, are in the world. 'Just a waitress'? My God, woman, you're in the trenches of sales and marketing. You're front-line public relations. You have faith in my work and an incredible sense of creative possibilities." In conclusion, I insisted, "You, my dear, *must* be my agent."

With that letter I enclosed my newly finished image, *Girl in the Mirror*. More than a gift, it was my way of telling her to look closely at her own reflection to see her own potential.

Inspired by my confidence in her, Melanie wrote to me over the next several weeks about her marketing ideas and her research into the category of art that my work apparently belonged in—"outsider art," as she told me it was called, the art of obsessively creative self-taught artists. I laughed at the name and the notion of being on the outside—a phrase that had its own special connotation in prison lingo. From that standpoint, I was as much an "insider" as one can be. But I was delighted at her enthusiasm for promoting my work, and we shared page after page of correspondence about our prospects. The initially reluctant Melanie quickly proved to be a fountain of advice as to how my new career might be advanced. She had taken up my challenge and was more than a match for it.

In December she wrote with news. She had paid a visit to the Albany Institute of History and Art, "dressed to the nines," as she put it, and approached the curator of the institute's Norman Rice Gallery with an attaché case full of my work. She must have done a very good job in making her pitch, because the curator was "astounded" by my stitcheries, in her words, and he immediately began making plans to include some of my art in a spring exhibit simply titled *Peace*. Even more exhilarating than the news about my work's acceptance for an exhibition was another announcement Melanie made in the same letter: She would soon be coming to visit me.

Since she had neither a driver's license nor a car at the time, Melanie had to arrange for a friend to bring her to Somers—a one-hundred-mile drive from Albany. We finally had our first face-to-face meeting in January 1991. As I moved through the doorway and metal detector that led into the large visiting room, I saw an enchanting, petite young woman in blue jeans, a white blouse, and a cardigan sweater. Her long chestnut hair swept around her softly, and her eyes sparkled with intensity. No sooner had our eyes met than we broke into wide smiles and spoke each other's names. In that moment, my consciousness of guards, bars, cement walls, and coils of razor wire was swept away, because there, in front of me, was the woman I'd dreamed of. For four months I had loved her letters, her words, and the spirit they conveyed. I had loved the sound of her voice on the two or three occasions I'd talked with her on the phone. And now, at last, I could love her physical presence as well. I had the strong impression that Melanie was equally taken up in the moment. Amid the tension of that instant, there was a magical sense of relief.

"Over there," said the visiting-room guard, gesturing. "Table next to the window."

We had an hour. Facing each other across the table, both of us smiling nervously, we swapped witticisms and tried to catch up on a lifetime of conversation. We had no trouble talking with each other, even though the surroundings made Melanie feel uneasy, she admitted. She had never before been inside a prison of any kind, and we were sitting in a sterile, colorless room furnished only with five rows of institutional tables with chairs on either side. I apologized for the less-than-romantic ambience, and we laughed. Melanie introduced the subject of the *Peace* exhibit.

"This is really quite exciting, Ray" she said. "The gallery is a prestigious place, quite top-shelf. It's a wonderful venue for the first showing of your work. I hope you're happy."

I assured her I was.

"Oh," she quickly added, "and are you ready for this? I made friends with a woman who has a connection at the local NBC affiliate. I'm going to get you TV coverage!" She smiled broadly.

"I'm going to be on television?" I asked, feeling slightly uncomfortable.

Melanie immediately read my misgivings. "It isn't exactly in the bag yet," she admitted. "But I feel that you have a wonderful talent. And . . ." She paused, clearing her throat to make light of the moment, then continued: "As your agent, I feel it's time to share your art with the world."

Reaching across the table, I placed my hand on top of Melanie's. "You're beautiful," I said softly. She blushed.

"Materson," bellowed a guard who had stepped up behind Melanie. "Time's up."

The moment was past, but the spell wasn't broken. We rose from our seats, keeping our eyes fixed on each other.

"You're beautiful, too, Ray," Melanie whispered.

As the steel door to the visiting room closed behind her, Melanie turned and offered a small wave. "I'll see you again," she mouthed as I lost sight of her. Those silent words stayed with me as I returned to my cage.

"I'll see you again."

27. EXCHANGE WITH A HUSTLER

Cesar Cruz, better known on the cell block as CC, had come to Somers a few months before I received my first letter from Melanie. A young man with broad shoulders, a round face, and a Fu Manchu mustache, he had been convicted of brutally killing his fiancée and had narrowly avoided the death penalty by making a last-minute plea of insanity. The jurors had apparently agreed with his attorney's contention that anyone who would kill his girlfriend and then strangle her dog to death must be at least slightly off center. He was sentenced to life without parole.

On the block, CC became known as a hustler, jokester, and part-time Bible toter. He had the slick personality of a used-car salesman but was generally easy to get along with. He was also a big fan of my artwork, and every day he would stop by my cell to see how my latest piece was progressing. Even during lock time—the hours when all inmates were locked in their cells for counts and shift changes—CC almost always managed to talk the guards into letting him roam. Moving from cell to cell, he swapped small talk and rumors with the other inmates, and he also cut deals for cigarettes and bars of soap. When he visited me, he would listen intently as I told him the stories behind the pieces I was working on. He always offered suggestions, and sometimes he brought me pairs of socks that other inmates had given him in exchange for loose smokes or state-issued packs of tobacco. He seemed to have connections everywhere, and even those inmates who talked hatefully about him behind his back took him up on sports bets and commissary deals.

"Hey, Mat," he whispered one afternoon, his smiling face pushed up against my cell bars. "Hey, I got a deal for you. Come here."

I got up from my bunk and stepped over to the bars. "What's going on?" I asked.

"Hey, listen. You're cool, right? I want to ask you a favor."

"I'm listening," I responded.

"I want you to make one of your pictures for me," he said, still whispering.

"I'm really busy getting it together for this show in Albany, New York," I told him.

"Yeah, well, it doesn't have to be like right now. But I want to pay you with these," he said, holding his hand open to display three thin marijuana joints. "Here, take them."

Without thinking, almost as if I were suddenly someone else, I let him drop the joints into my hand. I said, "Yeah, but . . ."

"I'll be back later to tell you what I want," he interrupted, walking away before I could say anything else.

I immediately wrapped the joints in a piece of paper and stuffed them into the binding of a book that I laid inconspicuously among a few other books. I told myself that this was okay, everything was cool, and I had nothing to worry about. I picked up my embroidery work-in-progress, a piece for the Rice Gallery exhibition, and resumed stitching.

The theme for the exhibit—"Peace"—seemed incongruous in view of my own circumstances and the state of the larger world. Operation Desert Shield was under way in the Middle East and was receiving prominent coverage in the news. The nation seemed to be preparing for war against Iraq, a country whose ruler was portrayed as a crazed, fanatical, cold-blooded killer. Peace in that part of the world continued to be as implausible as it did in the Somers state prison.

The image I happened to be working on that day was a portrait of a woman helicopter pilot whose story had aired on a recent TV news program. She had been moved to the Persian Gulf as part of the U.S. military buildup of forces there. She was proud to be serving her country, and her story had touched and inspired me. In her dedicated countenance and strong words I had felt the same strength that I'd known as a child when I'd first heard John Kennedy's words "Ask not what your country can do for you; ask what you can do for your country." I felt proud to be an American.

But even as a sense of nationalism pervaded my spirit, another conflicting theme whispered to me from the book binding where I'd stashed the joints. I remembered the parties, the times of abandon and euphoric oblivion, the sweetly pungent smell of marijuana as the smoke filled my lungs. I struggled against these thoughts. But ultimately they won out, and as the evening approached I found myself unwrapping the small package and removing one of the tightly wound bones, as they were called.

I checked the tier with my small Plexiglas-faced mirror. I scanned up and down to see that no guards or nosy inmates were wandering too near my cage. No one in either direction. Then I quickly moved to the back of my cell and, standing close to the small vent that was situated on the wall above the sink-toilet unit, I lit the joint. The smell was unmistakable. I sucked the smoke hard and deep into my lungs. There I held it, stifling an urge to cough. After a moment, I released my smoky breath slowly into the vent holes. I took another hard pull and watched as the tiny cigarette burned like a fuse closer to my fingers and lips. The taste was hot, harsh, and I relished it. This, I thought in the moment, could be the best of all possible worlds; I could have my art and I could have my former escape as well. The idea provoked me to near laughter as I drew another breath of smoke. But the thought was interrupted when I heard a noise from somewhere down the block. It was the sound of keys clinking together!

My giddy thoughts instantly transformed into hazy paranoia. The drug was potent. I doused the stub with spit and quickly put it into my mouth and swallowed it. Then I grabbed a plastic container of talcum powder and shot a small blast of it into the dormant air of the cell. I lit a cigarette and hopped onto my bunk as the sound of boots against the cement floor of the tier moved closer. Holding the cigarette somewhat shakily between my teeth, I reached for my sewing hoop. I was trying to focus on it as I held it upside down. My twisted anxiety and fear shot to greater heights as I heard Corrections Officer Manning's voice.

"Break seventy-three," came the call.

The familiar clack of my cell door as it was unlocked sounded surreal and filled me with dread. It occurred to me in my paranoid frame of mind that CC might have passed the joints to me to set me up for a bust. I couldn't understand why he might do that, but I was aware that such things often happened in prison. It's a game to some inmates. Maybe CC thought I looked too comfortable and wanted me to take a fall.

Manning pushed open the door of my cell and entered with another guard, a new-jack who looked like he was barely out of his teens. The youngster gazed at me suspiciously; then his eyes swept my cell and scanned my belongings. A torrent of cynical, smart-ass remarks came to mind as I studied the rookie in his crisply pressed uniform. But I restrained myself from speaking them, knowing they were induced by the dose of THC that was coursing through my brain.

"Hey, Mattie. What's new?" the guard asked in a conversational tone.

"Nothing much . . . biding my time," I stammered, having decided to remain lying on my bunk.

"You meet Mr. Fields yet?" he asked.

"N-no. Not officially, Mr. Manning," I responded in a voice that I hoped sounded like my normal tone.

"Well, I just wanted to show him one of your pictures. What are you working on?"

I handed him the sewing hoop, and as he leaned closer I looked away, feigning that I was sorting through the improvised spools of thread that lay scattered about my bunk. I had no desire to make eye contact with the guard, for I was certain mine would stand out like red neon.

"It's a picture of a soldier. A woman pilot over in the Persian Gulf. Saw her on TV," I remarked with words that sounded too staccato as they rang back into my ears.

"Look at this, Jeff," said the senior guard as he took hold of my hoop and moved toward the new-jack. "Isn't this amazing?"

Mr. Fields looked at the needlework with little display of enthusiasm and mumbled something.

"Nice work, Mattie. Keep it up," said Manning. He turned to the other guard and motioned for him to exit the cell. "Never have to worry about Materson." Then, protégé in tow, he left and shut my cell door.

I breathed a sigh of relief as the scenario played out in my mind and replayed like a video loop. A sinister thought ran through my mind: "You got one over on them." And I picked up my hoop and looked at it. I wanted to climb back into the image, into the feeling it had evoked in me. But in that instant I realized I could not. I understood right then and there, and quite unequivocally, that I could not have both worlds. I had to choose.

Realizing what might have happened if the guards had subjected me to a shakedown instead of a friendly visit, I became furious with myself and with the smooth-talking CC. I remembered my sweats and tremors when I was first arrested and how my system had cleansed itself of the poison I'd pumped into it. I considered the shame I had brought to myself and my family.

Then, disregarding the sure knowledge that I'd have to pay CC back, I took the remaining two joints he had entrusted me with and flushed them down the toilet. I felt triumphant. Free. And finally, with the artwork I'd decided to title *Major Mom* nestled next to my head on my pillow, I went to sleep. The next day, when CC made his customary visit to my cell, I paid him a carton of cigarettes for the bones he'd tossed me.

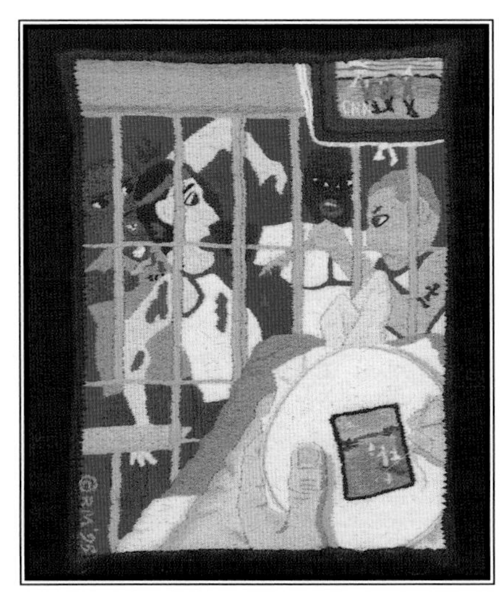

Less than a week later, there were loud cries and sounds of a scuffle out on the tier. Armed with at least one shank and a few mop-handle clubs, several gang members ambushed CC while the guards were searching another area of the cell block. It took only seconds for the assailants to cut and bludgeon his head, neck, back, and chest. Leaving him for dead, they retreated from the scene as quickly as they'd moved in. The guards, usually quick in responding to fights, watched from several feet away as CC moaned and convulsed on the hard cement walkway. Moments later, infirmary staff members entered the block, accompanied by the goon squad and a stretcher. The rest of us were locked down and secured as the unconscious body of Cesar Cruz was wheeled away.

28. An Eagle in Flight

Melanie hadn't neglected to tell me that she was married. Pouring out her soul to me in lengthy, heart-wrenching letters, she wrote of her marriage to her husband, Paul. She described how her initial love for him and her optimism about the relationship had gradually evaporated in their first couple of years together, during which they'd moved from place to place. Although Paul was an intelligent, hardworking man who did lighting and sound for concerts, she explained, their mutual zest for partying had destroyed the sense of loving trust they had once shared. The only remaining tie that connected them, she told me, was their love for their six-year-old son, John.

John's birth had been foretold, Melanie wrote, by the nesting of cardinals in a tree outside her bedroom window. When John was born, in the fall of 1984, his head was crowned with red hair. But when the birds abandoned their nests, Melanie told me, Paul began to seem increasingly distant, and that's when she took to drinking on an almost daily basis.

She cherished John and hoped to have more children. She'd committed herself to sobriety on several occasions, but each time she'd lapsed back into her drinking routine, feeling that Paul offered little support for her attempts at self-control. Nonetheless, they remained married.

She hoped she could free herself from the compulsion to drink. But the rooms of Alcoholics Anonymous felt threatening to her, and the anonymity that was assumed seemed tenuous. Still, she needed to talk, to share her pain and her shame with someone.

"You," she wrote to me, "are my last hope for sobriety."

"RAY, IT'S ABSOLUTELY WRONG for you to become emotionally involved with a woman who's married," Pastor Bert pronounced.

"But he's moved out, Bert—he's left her. And it isn't as though I'm running around with her," I somewhat sarcastically countered.

"Perhaps not," he said. "But if things were different, if you weren't where you are, then do you think you'd be 'running around'?"

"I can't say that I wouldn't be," I answered with some shame.

"Very well, then," he said, having made his point. "Listen, I appreciate that Melanie is helping you with your artwork. I appreciate that she's a supportive friend during this difficult time in your life. But marriage is a sacred union. Frequently the Lord tries marriages in ways we don't comprehend, only to strengthen them."

"But I love her, Bert," I said, almost whining.

"Ray, you must not encourage her to divorce," he concluded, "even if the husband has moved out."

As the visiting-room guard motioned that our time was up, Pastor Bert took my hands and offered a prayer. He appealed to the Lord to guide me, and to lead me into healing relationships. His words didn't sit well with me, but I prayed with him anyway, asking only for Melanie's happiness.

The *Peace* exhibit was on for several weeks in the spring of 1991. True to her word, Melanie had managed to generate television-news coverage of the show. One of the local stations had sent camera crews to the gallery and aired a short segment about a prison-inmate artist in Somers, Connecticut.

Over the next several months, Melanie and I continued to correspond, and she visited me as often as she could talk one of her friends into driving her to Somers and back. It wasn't easy, but I kept my promise to Pastor Bert, taking care to avoid offering any advice to Melanie regarding her strained marital relationship. Melanie was maintaining her sobriety, and she told me that was in large part because representing my artwork left her little time for hanging out in bars. She and I shared two copies of a daily devotional booklet, and I felt that our prayers were always offered together, even though our circumstances kept us apart.

I continued to sew my miniature creations. On receiving each new piece, Melanie responded with enthusiasm. We thrived on each other's encouragement. She sent me copies of the letters she had written on my behalf promoting my work. She also sent me socks, magazines, and the names of people to whom she had spoken about me. One of these people was Ann

Gati, an art teacher in Albany who liked my work. Ann regularly vacationed in New Mexico, and Melanie asked her to show some of my pieces to curators at the Museum of International Folk Art in Santa Fe. It was a big step, Melanie assured me—not only a potential sale, but also the first time she was "letting the babies go off on their own." I understood, and for the next few weeks, we waited for news from Ann Gati.

It was around that time that I was approached about making a special piece by a fellow inmate whose last name was Sallie, but who was invariably referred to as "Scabby." The nickname was inspired by the numerous sores on his body. He was a former junkie who had been diagnosed as having AIDS, and his obvious illness tended to keep people at a distance. He became even more isolated after his hair started falling out. During meals, he could regularly be seen sitting alone at a table in the otherwise crowded mess hall.

One day he came up to my cell with a magazine in his hand. "Hey, Ray, man," he began, "I know you're a really busy guy. I think that's cool. You're the only knucklehead around here who's got anything going on."

"Thanks, I guess," I responded lightly.

"Well, look, I got this magazine here. It's got this picture of an eagle in it, and, well, the eagle's my symbol." He held the magazine open for me to see the photograph he was talking about. He continued, "I was wondering if you could make one of your pictures for me. Of this eagle."

I looked at the photo of the majestic bird, its wings outstretched as it soared against a background of mountains and redwood trees. It was a strong, beautiful, stately image. Then I looked at the pitiful man holding the magazine. His body was pale and emaciated, gray in spots, and his eyes were sunken and ringed with dark circles. I tried to imagine him as an eagle, but I couldn't.

"Hey, will you make this for me?" he asked again. "I know you could do it. It would mean a lot to me, man."

"Leave the magazine," I told him. "I'll try to get to it."

"Thanks, Ray," he said, "thanks a lot," and he walked away pleased.

A week after that, before I'd even picked up the magazine from where I'd left it, a gurney was brought down from the hospital, and Sallie was taken away. He died about two weeks later, quietly and in his sleep, I heard. Picking up the magazine and thumbing to the picture of the eagle, I wondered if Sallie had finally gotten his wings.

Accustomed to getting a letter from Melanie almost every other day, I began to worry when I didn't hear from her in nearly a week. Then my door clacked open one Monday afternoon.

"Materson. Visit," said the guard.

I pulled on my best visiting uniform, quickly brushed my teeth, and stepped out of my cell. After closing the door behind me, I headed down the tier to pick up a visiting-room pass. Melanie didn't generally travel to Somers on Mondays, but I still hoped it was her. I walked quickly along the right side of the yellow line painted on the floor of the main prison corridor. Stopping at the control cage, I showed my pass and was cleared to step into the next corridor. At the end, I found Melanie sitting in the waiting area and waving to me.

After what seemed an interminable wait for the steel doors to be opened and shut, we finally met with a brief embrace in the visiting room; then we were led to a table, where, as always, we sat across from each other. Melanie was beaming.

"I don't know where to begin," she said.

"I haven't heard from you in a week," I said hastily.

"Well, just cool your jets," she retorted. "It isn't like I've been taking a vacation. I'm busy like you can't believe out there."

"Yeah, I know," I told her, "but I worry."

"Well, just stop worrying and listen for a minute." She held her hand up. "Okay," she asked, "are you ready?"

"Yes."

"Remember my friend Ann Gati, who I told you about?" she asked, quickly adding, "And don't you dare ask me if she's any relation to John Gotti."

"I won't."

"Well, she's come through for us in spades," she said, her eyes sparkling. "She sold three pieces of your work to the museum in New Mexico."

I leaned forward in my chair, about to speak.

"But wait," she continued. "That's not all. When Ann called me at the beginning of last week with the news, I wrote some press releases and sent them out. By the way, you're going to have to buy me a new typewriter pretty darn soon. I'm wearing out the keys."

"Not a problem," I said anxiously.

"Okay. Well, anyway, guess who thinks your story is the hottest thing since sliced bread? I'll tell you who: the Associated Press," she bubbled.

"*The* Associated Press?" I asked.

"There's only one that I know of." She laughed. "So, they're going to be contacting the prison to arrange for an interview with you. They're even going to send a photographer. You're going to get national coverage, bucko!"

"Wild!" I said, feeling a bit nervous.

"Hey," she asked, "what's the matter? You don't seem half as thrilled as I'd expected." Then, in a more settled tone, she added, "Oh, and there's one more matter."

"I-I'm sorry," I stammered. "All this just seems . . . Well, it's hard for me to take it all in."

"Paul and I are divorcing," she stated in a matter-of-fact tone.

Remembering my promise to Bert, I asked, "Are you sure this is what you want?"

"Am I sure?" Melanie asked, clearly angered by my question. "Well, what do you think—that the idea just suddenly occurred to me as I walked through the door of this lovely place? Jeez! First I get this deadpan response to the best news your fledgling art career has ever had, then you're questioning me on a divorce decision that I've been wrestling with for, well, a damn long time! I ought to just leave! I should have written all this to you." With that, she began to cry.

I felt awful—useless. "Hey," I pleaded, "I'm really sorry!"

"You should be sorry," she sobbed, wiping tears from her face with the sleeve of her blouse.

"I guess it's just a lot of news," I said, trying to explain my somewhat confused feelings. "I told you I was worried about you. I didn't know if it was going to be you here today or not. Plus I've been trying really hard not to influence you either way on your relationship with Jack."

Calming herself, Melanie replied, "Ray, Jack and I haven't had a relationship in years. Getting a formal divorce is something we both have simply put off. Can we move back to the happier news, please?"

"It's great news, Mel," I assured her. "I can't thank you enough for all the work you've been doing."

"Sure you can," she said with a twinkle in her eye. "But not until you get out of here."

We talked about all that had happened during the previous week, and Melanie offered some encouragement and advice regarding the Associated Press interview. She told me that such things take time to arrange. "So don't be sitting on pins and needles waiting for the press corps," she said as the guard walked toward us. Our time was up for this visit.

At the door we embraced and kissed. Melanie's lips were warm and soft against mine. Assured in that moment that fairy tales can indeed come true, I had never felt more in love. I wandered back to D Block, euphoric.

• • •

29. BIG G OF J-3

Gino Calli was an exceptionally large man known to almost everyone as "Big G." Rumors about him abounded—that he had been a hit man for the mob, that he had engineered major armored-car heists, that in his younger days he had been a professional wrestler and the leader of a notorious biker gang. None of these stories were true, as it turned out, but they served to create a mystique and gave other inmates a rich topic on which to speculate. I met Big G in the fall of 1991, when I was finally moved from TTU into the J section of the prison.

The J section was a grouping of four separate cell blocks located on the opposite side of the prison from the D and F Blocks. Like the maximum-security blocks, they were two-tiered buildings, but they contained larger cells than the other blocks, and each cell had its own window looking out over the yard. Because everyone assigned to the J section was expected to have a job in the prison—the lowly, nominal position of window washer, if nothing else—there was considerably more freedom of mobility, and the cell doors were almost always left open. For all of these reasons, the J's were commonly referred to as the prison "condos." The downside to the J's was that half of the cells were for two-man occupancy. As a new kid on the block, I was assigned to one of the two-man cells.

I arrived at my new home, J-3, cell thirteen, early one afternoon to find the block almost completely deserted, except for Big G and two cell-block tiermen. The three stood together and watched as I walked to my cell carrying two green plastic trash bags that contained the sum total of my earthly possessions. I'd had to leave my loaner TV in D Block, but I had been assured that I could apply for a new one after I was settled into my new "house." In any case, I wasn't too concerned about it. I had realized that television was just as addictive as drugs.

Wondering about my new cellmate, I surveyed the domain we would be sharing in J-3, cell thirteen. The steel toilet bowl–sink unit was at the foot of the wall-mounted steel bunk beds. My cellmate's bunk—the lower one, of course—was tightly made up and connected at the foot to a built-in steel shelf that held a color television. Against the wall opposite the bunks, there was an industrial-looking metal desk unit with an attached metal stool. The desktop contained a small stack of magazines, writing materials, and a blue coffee mug. Everything looked clean and was neatly arranged.

I began unpacking my things and noticed the posters along the walls. Two were centerfold pullouts from a biker magazine—big color images of large-breasted, scantily clad young women provocatively posed with Harley-Davidson motorcycles. Another poster featured the heavy-metal rock group Metallica. Also on one wall was a document that bore a Nazi SS logo and, below it, lines of text with the heading PLEDGE OF THE ARYAN BROTHERHOOD. After perusing the first few hate-promoting lines, I turned away, filled with foreboding. Then the door rolled open, and in stepped Sonny Crandall.

A muscular, blond-haired man of medium height, he moved toward his bunk and tore off a dirty T-shirt to reveal numerous tattoos, including another SS logo. "So who the hell are you?!" he spat.

"Guess I'm your new cellmate," I said, holding out my hand. "Name's Ray."

"No, your name's Gone," he shot back disdainfully, pulling on a black Harley-Davidson T-shirt and hurrying back out the door. A string of obscenities echoed through the cell block as Sonny let everyone within earshot know how he felt about having a new cellmate. I was nervous and frightened, and I whispered a rather disjointed prayer for my safety.

It's been said that the Lord hears all prayers, but that sometimes his answer is no, and sometimes it's "Wait a while." And then there are times when it's . . .

"Hi. Gino Calli's my name."

The big man literally filled the cell doorway, grinning through his dark, heavy beard. He stuck out a huge hand, and I moved toward him and offered a greeting.

"Gotta forgive young Sonny there," Gino chuckled. "He flunked social-graces class. He'll get over it."

"Yeah, I hope so," I muttered. "I don't like to get off on the wrong foot."

"You're the sewing guy, right?" he asked.

"That's me," I answered, relaxing a bit.

"I've seen your work. You did some flags for Miguel Sanchez. Miguel houses over in J-2. I'll let him know you've checked in." He smiled tentatively.

As the big man turned to leave, Sonny walked up behind him. "My man, Big G! What's happenin'?" he gushed with phony sentiment. Then, looking at me, he complained, "They moved this punk loser into my house, Big G. I ain't about no cellmates."

"You'll get along okay," Gino assured my new cellmate. "Ray here sews. Did the Puerto Rican flags for Miguel Sanchez." Then he turned to me and said, "Talk to you later, Ray. Maybe I'll have some work for you."

As Gino lumbered away, Sonny remarked, almost phrasing it as a question, "So you're Big G's boy."

"We've met," I said.

"What's this about sewing?" asked the young rowdy as he once again began pulling his shirt off, in a proud display of his well-developed physique.

Trying to appear unshaken by his initial hostility, I pulled my embroidery hoop from the bag I was unpacking, and I showed him an image that I had recently begun stitching. A threaded needle dangled from the hoop. "This is what I do," I said.

Sonny took a quick look at the work-in-progress. "Oh, Christ!" he screeched. "Please tell me you're not a faggot!"

"No," I said.

"Well, at least you ain't a nigger." He smiled and slapped me hard on the shoulder. "Long as you're cool, we'll be all right."

SHARING A CELL WITH SONNY might have been a very difficult experience had it not been for Big G, who turned out to be a great admirer of my work. He continually asked me what I was working on, and with very few words to that effect, he made it clear that he preferred that the other inmates leave me alone. Once, when I was working on a Shakespeare image, Gino made arrangements with one of the guards to bring a VCR into his cell, along with a videotape of a recent movie treatment of *Hamlet,* starring Mel Gibson. Then he invited me over for an afternoon screening. We enjoyed talking about the film and the story, and we also enjoyed gobbling down two boxes of Little Debbie chocolate cakes—a confection that Big G seemed to relish greatly. I quickly came to value Gino's company. A good conversationalist, he disdained the standard jailhouse banter and rumormongering in favor of discussing life, ideas, and the future. Not that his own future held anything but the promise of continued prison time.

When I met Big G, he had already been incarcerated for seventeen years. As a young man who partied heavily and abused drugs, he had participated in a robbery that left several innocent people dead. Gino would say very little about the incident, but I came to understand that he was highly remorseful for his actions and haunted by memories of the killings. As I sat listening to him talk of his dreams—trout fishing, living in a secluded north-country cabin, and learning to be a falconer—I found it hard to believe that this man was a murderer. It seemed all the more unfathomable when I saw him walking to a Bible-study group, his huge hand clutching his tiny prayer book.

30. A Demon in the House

Corrections Officer Brink had removed several old notices from the cell-block bulletin board and was tacking up a few new ones. The badly photocopied sheets of paper announced chapel schedules, inmate job postings, and classification hearings. I had been taking a break from sewing—a regular necessity, for the sake of my eyes—and decided to check out the latest announcements. There was one for the annual Indian Corn Festival, a religious event held in the cafeteria each fall, and another announcing the Catholic confession schedule for October. There was also a sheet of paper with the heading BOARD OF PARDONS.

I had heard about the state Board of Pardons almost from the day I'd arrived at Somers. Since regulations specified that prisoners would be considered for pardons only after they'd served a minimum of four years, I'd simply filed away the notion of applying to the board in the back of my mind. As I read the notice, I mentally counted the years during which I'd been a guest of the state. My spirit leaped when I suddenly realized that by February, in only a few months, I would meet the minimum time-served criterion. I quickly walked to the block officer's desk to request phone time.

Overcome with a sense of urgency, I repeatedly dialed Melanie's phone number. Each time, there was the hollow, distant sound of ringing, but no cheery "Hello" at the other end of the line. Not that I was surprised. Since it was only two in the afternoon, Melanie was almost certainly at work—"slinging hash," as she liked to put it—at the upscale University Club in

Albany. As I stood cradling the phone against my shoulder, my cellmate, Sonny, breezed past me on his way back from work, giving me a punch in the left arm that seemed a little harder than a friendly jab.

"I'll be on the can," he announced curtly as he glanced over his shoulder. Then he added, "Don't bother me."

Sonny seemed to spend an inordinate amount of time "on the can," but I willingly afforded him his privacy, and he generally returned the favor. After three years of using the toilet in something of a fish-bowl atmosphere, I coveted and appreciated simple moments of privacy. Still, I had my suspicions about Sonny.

"Hey, what's up, Ray?" inquired Gino Calli as he strode up beside me.

"Trying to get a call through to Melanie," I briefly explained to the big man. "Pardons board."

"Yeah," he chuckled. "Well, I wish you good luck."

"You familiar with the process?" I asked him.

"Brother," he responded, "after the first six tries at getting in to see the board, I gave up. 'Bout six years ago. I used to think it was just me, but the truth is, in seventeen years I can't think of anybody that's received a pardon. Politics," he concluded. As he turned and slowly moved back to his cell, he added, "Don't much care for politics."

Big G's remarks hit me hard. Maybe the whole notion of being pardoned was a farce. Still, I reminded myself that my crimes were fairly tame compared to multiple homicide. The thought didn't sit well with me, I realized as I noticed my reflection in the metal phone housing. Staring back at me was a criminal who was no less guilty than anyone else in the prison, and it occurred to me that this was how the system and the larger world viewed me. I dialed Melanie's phone number again and let it ring. When there was no answer, I wandered back to J-3, cell thirteen, overcome with a strange feeling of defeat. Momentarily forgetting Sonny's request of only a few minutes earlier, I automatically rolled open the cell door.

"Hey! What the—?! Get the hell outta here!!" fumed Sonny. He was sitting on the end of his bunk, a red handkerchief tied around the top of his arm and a hypodermic syringe hanging from a bulging vein below it. I rolled the door back open and stepped hurriedly away, but the image was already seared into my brain.

I began walking up to Big G's cell, my mind filled with thoughts that tore at one another. After being unable to get through to Melanie, and upon hearing Gino's gloomy assessment of my prospects with the Board of Pardons, I had already felt depressed enough. But to find Sonny in the cell shooting up was too much. The spike in his arm beckoned to me at the same time it terrified me. Drugs had been my solace for years. They had made me feel good and had temporarily eliminated the pain of the world. At that moment, I felt like I needed some pain medication. It was an unpleasant feeling.

"You look like you've seen a ghost," remarked Big G when I showed up at his cell door.

"That's the way I feel," I said.

"So, what's up?" he asked.

I entered his crowded cell and sat on his footlocker. "Sonny," I said. "Sonny's down in the house shooting dope, man."

"Oh, for. . . . He ain't learned," muttered the big man. "Don't know what you can do about it. That's Sonny's demon."

"Yeah," I said, "it's his demon until the house gets shaken down and I get pulled into it. Damn! I've been working hard at avoiding trouble, G."

"I don't know what good it would do," said Gino, "but I'll talk to him if you want."

Gino rarely offered to intervene on behalf of anyone who was having a problem, although other inmates often conferred with him about how to handle difficult situations. I took some comfort in knowing that I had a good last resort, but the unwritten law in prison was that you settled your own scores. Thanking Gino for his generous offer, I advised him that I would try to "adjust things" on my own.

"Best way to do it," he confirmed. Then he added, "But don't get him mad. Dope has a bad tendency to bring out the crazy in people."

"Don't I know it!" I said as I left Gino's cell. "Don't I know it!"

What I didn't know, of course, was what kind of reception to expect from Sonny when I returned to my cell. There was no delaying that inevitable confrontation, because C.O. Brink was on the tier calling for inmates to lock up for the three o'clock count. So I walked back to J-3, thirteen, and strode in, locking the door behind me. Sonny was in his bunk and under the covers, watching cartoons.

"What's up, old man," he said, grinning.

"Nothing."

"Tough day at work for me," he said. "They got spaghetti at chow tonight. Don't think I can handle it."

It quickly became clear to me that he wanted to simply pretend I hadn't seen him injecting drugs into his arm. As long as I played along, everything would be fine. It occurred to me that the only thing missing was a perfect evening meal and my mom, puttering around with a dust cloth and saying, "Everything's fine. We have a beautiful roast and Dad's favorite potatoes."

Denial, like they say, is more than a river in Egypt.

Climbing up on my bunk, I resumed my sewing. As I tried to suppress a feeling that I was being cowardly in not calling Sonny on his behavior, a vivid image suddenly flashed into my mind.

Living through drug addiction is a spiritually degrading experience in which the whole of your existence becomes very narrowly defined. As an addict, I didn't care about anything —anything—but the next fix. Always underlying that feeling of anticipation was the sense that this time, somehow, the euphoria would last indefinitely, even forever. But just as sure as the high would arrive, it always evaporated after about ten minutes, leaving pain, misery, and trouble. With an addiction, you continually attempt to find the lasting high, again and again, until everything is gone in a downward-spiraling cycle. Christ told his disciples to leave everything behind, pick up a cross, and follow him. Addiction demands the same kind of sacrifice.

So while I was angry at Sonny and, to a lesser degree, myself, I couldn't help feeling sorry for him, because I knew something he didn't, and I realized that confrontational words wouldn't change that. Sitting on my bunk, I picked up a pad and began sketching the image that my reflective musings had inspired. It was a picture that seemed to summarize the horrors that drugs had brought into my life. Whether it would speak to Sonny, I didn't know.

"HOLY GOOD GOD!" SPOUTED GINO, staggering a half step backward, when I showed him the finished work on my sewing hoop.

"What do you think?" I asked him

"What do I think?!" he began. "This, my man, says it all! Anybody who ever walked the drug path knows what this is talking about. I gotta hand it to you, Ray. You've outdone yourself with this one," he said.

My new piece had gotten its first review. The big man had been moved. It was more than I'd expected when I began stitching the image, which I'd titled *Don't Get Pulled In.* In the background is a tight close-up of a demon's fiery red face, his wide eyes fixed on the hypodermic syringe and spoon in the immediate foreground. Instead of sucking up a liquid drug solution from the spoon, the syringe is literally pulling into it a tiny, terrified-looking human being who is struggling frantically to escape.

I couldn't help feeling a profound sense of accomplishment as Gino called a few other inmates over to see the piece. They immediately began talking, sharing their own experiences with addiction and the problems they had encountered in their attempts to kick it. I had made a statement, conveyed a message that touched people. I looked forward to showing the image to Sonny.

"So, what the hell is it?" Sonny irritably demanded as he looked past my embroidery hoop, half-hypnotized by the cartoon show on his television.

"It's me," I said.

"Ha!" he chuckled as he passed it back to me. "Guess I should've known by the skinny arms."

"Go ahead and yuk it up, Sonny," I said, "but drugs are the reason that I'm in this craphole. Drugs are the reason most everybody is here. Take a look around! You're an idiot if you don't see! A damn fool!" By this point, I was shouting.

"Well, ain't this a sight!" Sonny began as he quickly stood

up from his bunk. "Outta-shape old granny-man is gettin' her knittin' needles up! You got something you wanna say to me? You better be able to back it up, punk!"

"Yeah," I said, now face-to-face with him, "I got something to say. I'm working at staying clean. Drugs have done nothing but screwed up my life, and it doesn't help my sobriety to come into the cell and find you with a freaking spike in your arm. Plus, maybe you don't give a damn if you get nailed with contraband in the cell, but I do. I want out of here, not another court case. I've got some good things going on. And what really gets me is that you could have some good things happening for yourself if you didn't spend all your spare time looking for a fix!"

Sonny heatedly stared at me through narrowed eyes. He pumped up his chest and slammed his right fist into his left hand, making a loud smacking sound. "I could tear you apart, old man." He laughed, then quickly reached out toward me, wrapped his arms around my shoulders, and added, "But maybe I'll just make you my girl instead."

I felt so humiliated, stupid, and powerless that I was enraged. I wanted to hurt Sonny, but that wasn't my way, and I knew I was no match for him physically. So I spontaneously grabbed him under the ribs and began tickling him. Still trying to hold on to me, Sonny began giggling and telling me to stop. Then, suddenly, C.O. Brink's face appeared at the cell window for three o'clock count.

"Practicing for the prom, girls?" he asked in his usual monotone.

With that, Sonny let go of me, still laughing, then glanced at the door and said, "Yo, Brink! Don't get it messed up. It ain't nothin'."

"Nothin' I ain't seen before," Mr. Brink added as he moved, unaffected, away from the door and mechanically continued his task.

Sonny turned back toward me and said, "You're a punk and an idiot!"

"No, Sonny, you da punk. I was leading," I smirked. Then I had to duck a roll of toilet paper he threw at me.

With the tension dispelled, Sonny and I talked for the first time since I'd moved into the cell with him. Reading between the lines as I listened to him, I could tell that Sonny carried a great deal of shame. The son of uneducated immigrant parents, he had been severely beaten by both his parents and his older brother. At an early age, Sonny had taken to the streets in his ghetto neighborhood. Drugs, gangs, and crime came to dominate his life, pushing far into the background his talent for drawing and his interest in writing poetry. He was thirteen when he was first arrested and sentenced to serve time in a juvenile lockup facility. It was there that he was indoctrinated with the racist jargon and philosophy of the Aryan Brotherhood.

"But you know, Ray," he confided, "my best friend in the neighborhood is black. I don't really believe in any of this stuff." He gestured toward the poster that had caught my attention soon after I'd walked into the cell for the first time.

Sonny ended up talking at great length that afternoon about

his life, his insecurities, and his fears. He made us coffee and dipped into his secret stash of Hostess fruit pies, which we ate for dinner that evening instead of going to the cafeteria. He showed me his drawings, which he'd kept hidden in the bottom of his footlocker. Many of them were cartoonish, and some featured racist caricatures and sentiments that reflected white-supremacist ideology. He explained each one of those with a timid, passing apology and moved quickly to others that he took pride in.

It was an enlightening experience listening to Sonny that afternoon, and our talk left me with the feeling that a close friendship was in the making. Finally, as we climbed into our separate bunks that night, Sonny told me that he didn't keep any drugs in the cell, and he promised that he wouldn't shoot up in our house anymore.

31. Denied and Transferred

"The image just cries out to be an antidrug poster," Melanie said to me over the phone a few hours after she'd received my most recent letter and enclosure—my *Don't Get Pulled In* piece. Although she was uncertain about where to turn to make that idea a reality, she said she was determined to make it happen.

We also discussed the Board of Pardons and she adopted a cautiously hopeful approach. "I think we absolutely have to give it a try," she said. "But I also think your friend Gino might be right. People appointed to government boards tend to be less than liberal, especially when it comes to prisons. Nobody is too enthusiastic about championing the cause of a convicted felon." Then she added, "Except perhaps me."

Over the next several weeks, I wrote letters to virtually everyone I knew—old friends, former employers, college professors who I hoped would remember me, and fellow members of the Avery Street Christian Reformed Church. During that same period, I met with the church's new pastor, Doug Vander Wall. Bert had left to pastor another congregation near Seattle, and his departure had saddened me. But I liked Pastor Doug, a tall man whose demeanor was more formal than Bert's. He assured me that he'd do what he could to persuade people at the church to write letters of support as we prepared to petition the Board of Pardons.

In addition to working a full-time job and tending to her son, Melanie took on the monumental task of finding reasonably priced legal assistance to help with the petition, and she began orchestrating her plan to transform my embroidered statement about drug abuse into a poster. She also managed to get a car and a driver's license, and to keep up her frequent correspondence with me.

The Christmas season came and went. Pastor Doug and I began to develop a strong relationship, and other members of the church also visited me regularly. Melanie had brought the idea of the anti-drug-abuse poster to the director of the Connecticut Sports Museum, a man who also did curatorial work for the Aetna Art Gallery in Hartford. He quickly became caught up in her enthusiasm, along with Sam Connor, the co-ordinator of the Connecticut Prison Association. It was a productive alignment of people and resources.

There was also a lot of excitement over the nationally syndicated Associated Press article about me, which appeared in December 1991 and brought me letters from all over the country. One woman wrote and said that she had thought for a long time about embarking on an art career, and that reading about my "sock art" had inspired her to finally do it. Another wrote to say that the article gave her hope at a difficult time in her life. Letters from several elderly ladies were accompanied by bags and boxes of embroidery supplies that deteriorating eyesight kept them from using any longer. Prison regulations specified that I could be given materials only from individuals on my approved list of visitors, so the sewing supplies were donated to a local community arts and crafts program.

It was the encouragement I received from Melanie, the church, and these caring strangers that helped me face each day. I dreamed of finally being beyond the penitentiary walls, united with Melanie, and sharing laughter, love, and creative pursuits with her. I created dreamy images on my sewing hoop in anticipation of the pardon I believed I would soon be granted.

I was in for a hard reality check on that score. In April 1992, I received a letter that read, in full, "The Board of Pardons will not be reviewing your case. You will be eligible to reapply in one year."

I was crushed, devastated. I couldn't believe that my application, with all its letters of support and accompanying positive news articles about me, could have been dismissed with no more comment than that. I buried my face in my pillow and cried, while Sonny chuckled at his afternoon cartoons in the bunk below.

It wasn't until later that evening that I felt motivated to open the remaining pieces of mail I'd received that day. The first envelope I unsealed contained a card from Melanie, in which she told me to take heart and assured me that we would soon be together. In keeping with our agreement, we had spoken only reservedly of the application. Now that it was a moot issue, I anguished over how I would break the news to her, and I wondered if our love was strong enough to carry us through another year of separation. Melanie was young, gifted, witty, and stunningly pretty, and she was out in the world. My emotions were spent, and in that state, I was possessed by the hopeless feeling that I had little to offer her.

I went to sleep that night to the loud noises the goon squad was making as they worked to break into the nearby cell of a fellow inmate familiarly known as Crazy Bob. Drunk on home brew, he had locked himself in, and he spewed curses and insults at the guards as they struggled to spring the steel door. Finally, they maced him, broke through his makeshift door braces, and dragged him, naked, out of the cell. Drama from another planet.

I dreamed of beaches, open doors, and quiet, precious moments with my love.

Pastor Doug visited me the following day. His gentle smile and regal bearing never failed to give me comfort. That day, before I could explain my recent letdown, he began our meeting with news he hoped would cheer me.

"We've cleaned up our spare bedroom, and Melanie is going to spend the Easter weekend with us. She and John. She'll be able to visit you several times over a few days, and Leanne and I will have the opportunity to get to know her better, too."

"I got some news from the pardons board," I told him, without responding to what he had just said.

His face showed that he knew it wasn't favorable news. "I'm guessing it wasn't what you'd hoped for," he said.

"They turned me down." Anger and sadness welled up inside of me as I spoke the words. "Won't even be meeting with me," I added in a near whisper, and tears came to my eyes.

"I'm really so very sorry, Ray," he said, reaching across the table between us and taking my hands in his. Like the glowing countenance of Christ in an old prayer-book illustration, Doug's face radiated compassion and love. Without pausing, and maintaining a conversational tone, he offered a prayer. "Lord," he began, "we feel such disappointment in this moment and are overcome with sadness. Yet in this, too, we recognize that it is your will which leads and directs the course of our lives. Please be with Ray in this time and help him to see the wisdom of your ways. Open a new door, Father, and guide both Melanie and him through it. In Christ's name we pray. Amen."

There was a vestige of my soul that wanted to cry out in anger at the seeming inequity of "God's ways." But Doug had uttered his prayer with such confident sincerity that I was, at least momentarily, calmed. "I'm still very sad, Doug," I admitted. "I feel let down."

"I'm certain of that, Ray," he assured me. Then he added, "It may be a blessing that Melanie will be here this weekend. You can draw on each other for strength. Have more time together than usual, even as it is."

We spent the remainder of our time together in light conversation about relationships and projects I was planning.

"A time may come," said Doug, "when you will look back at this time and envy it. Few people can spend as much time as you do on creative pursuits."

"I will never miss this place," I said as I looked around the cold, sterile visiting room. Then, as always, our time drew to a seemingly premature close, and I was escorted to the room's inmate door, while Doug left by the visitors' exit.

After the mandatory frisk, I headed back to my cell. The visit with Pastor Doug had helped me, and I was comforted by the knowledge that Melanie was going to be around for the weekend. But as I arrived at my cell, I recognized my belongings on a steel cart that had been rolled up to the door. Sonny stood watching from a few steps away as two guards continued to move plastic trash bags full of my possessions out of the cell and onto the cart. When he saw me, he waved grotesquely and said, "See ya later, chump!"

I didn't understand what was happening until C.O. Pellitere walked up to me and explained it in a few words. "Can't go back into the block, Materson," he said, holding his arms out as if he were ready to stop me from bolting into the cell block. "You're being transferred."

Gino Calli lumbered up to survey the situation. "You're leaving us, my friend," he observed, his voice a little wistful.

"But what, what the hell, Gino?" I stammered. "Why are they moving me from the block?"

"It ain't the block," he said. "You're going to Minimum."

"Minimum?" I questioned, as my eyes moved back and forth from Big G to the guards, whose progress I was following as they emptied the cell of my things.

"Carl Robinson Correctional," he replied. "You'll know people there. Look up Joey Paca when you get over there. He'll hook you up. Good luck, Ray."

"G'bye, Granny," were the last words I heard from Sonny, who was clearly elated about my abrupt departure. So much for my illusion of friendship with him. But despite Sonny's enduring hostility, I had grown comfortable, and I didn't want to leave. I'd become accustomed to a routine that I had been left alone to pursue. Everyone in the prison—guards, administrators, and inmates—knew about my art and tolerated my working on it. I had no way of knowing how my embroidery and my huge collection of raw materials and supplies would be received at the new facility, and that question worried me tremendously.

As the guards in charge of my transfer led me down the long gray corridor, I saw Lieutenant Lawrence, who had been a line officer when I'd landed at Somers.

"Going to Carl Robinson, eh?" he greeted me.

"Yeah," I said, and added imploringly, "but I don't think I want to, Lieutenant."

"Well, you're on the list," he replied. "It's a good move, Ray. Says they're not afraid you're going to 'rabbit' anymore." He chuckled as he made that reference to the escape that had gained me some notoriety when I'd landed at Somers.

"But what about the artwork, sir?" I wondered.

"Not sure, Ray," he admitted. "But, look, do you remember Captain Belmont?"

Belmont had been the supervising captain of the transitional unit—a strict administrator, but also known for his fairness. Although I'd had little interaction with him, he had officially approved my interview with the Associated Press, and I guessed that he had informally approved of my art-making activities in general.

"Sure, I remember him," I said. "I don't know him that well, though."

"He'll remember you, Mattie," Lieutenant Lawrence assured me. "Anyway, he's deputy warden at Minimum now. Just moved over there a couple of weeks ago."

For the first time in more than three years, I was led through the gates of CCI at Somers, sporting one of the mandatory orange jumpsuits worn only by inmates being transferred from one institution to another. It was early evening, and the sky was clear. I was handcuffed and chained together with about a dozen other inmates, and we moved slowly down the walkway. At the guardhouse just inside the perimeter fences, a captain and a lieutenant compared our faces to those in the official inmate photographs they held. After being cleared at the guardhouse, we all struggled with our chains while climbing onto a white school bus. I noticed a bluebird painted above the doorway alongside the manufacturer's logo. Melanie, I thought, would read it as a favorable sign indeed!

32. Minimum

Carl Robinson Correctional Institution was roughly a mile and a half down the road from the maximum-security prison. The short trip there reminded me of my last ride on a school bus, which had been during a geology-class field trip while I was a student at Thomas Jefferson College. The trip had been cleverly billed as an Autumn Rock Festival, and I remembered the tie-dyed shirts and peace-symbol medallions that many of the students wore, and the sound of one of them playing folk music on an acoustic guitar that he'd brought along. I wondered what my former classmates would think of the Bluebird bus to Minimum.

"Yo, make sure they don't stick you in Building Five," muttered the Latin kid sitting next to me. "Lots of snitches and faggots."

I wondered how he would have such inside information, but I thanked him for the tip. Then he asked if I had a cigarette—payment for the advice, I reckoned. Nothing comes for free in prison, or on the prison bus.

The bus squeaked to a stop at the front entrance to the facility. There were no guard towers. Instead of the khaki uniforms that were standard at Somers, the inmates here wore green—the color of hope. As we clumsily filed off the bus, I looked back toward the prison where I had spent the last four years. The full moon rising over the prison water tower reminded me of a Eucharist host, and I suddenly felt like an orange-clad altar boy in a most unheavenly procession.

After being strip-searched and issued a set of CRCI greens, I was ushered around to the property room and the inmate-supplies building. I asked a few inmates if Joey Paca was around, but none of them seemed to know who I was talking about. An officer in the property room told me that my belongings would be searched over the next few days, and that I'd be allowed to keep anything that wasn't considered contraband. Needless to say, that worried me, because virtually all my art supplies could technically be considered contraband. This didn't exactly seem like a "door opening," as Pastor Doug had said.

The next stop in my introduction to Minimum was the Reception Unit in Building Six. At least I wouldn't have to worry about "snitches and faggots," I thought, feeling oddly relieved. Like all the units at CRCI, as I was to learn, the Reception Unit was simply a large room, a "dormitory," with forty sets of bunk beds arranged in four rows of ten. The more-coveted bunks were against the walls and were accompanied by stand-up lockers. Woolen blankets draped over some of the bottom bunks afforded minimal privacy for those bunks' occupants, but it was always short-lived, because guards would pull the blankets down whenever they made the rounds. At the foot of virtually every bunk, top and bottom, was a television set. In the evenings, men would sit on their bunks wearing headphones and tuned in to their favorite evening programs. As a new arrival, I didn't have a television, but watching my fellow prisoners as they stared catatonically into the gray TV light made me glad I didn't.

My bunkmate, Anthony, introduced himself, and I was pleased at his quiet, confident demeanor. A large, fortyish black man who was the tier man for our side of the dormitory, he was looking forward to release sometime in the next couple of months. He showed me pictures of his wife and children.

Explaining the unit's routine, he said, "Breakfast is at six o'clock, but you don't have to go if you don't want to. Make sure you get on the laundry list so you won't get hassled trying to do your wash. Before you leave for work in the morning, make sure your bunk is made, or you'll get written up. Phones get shut off at nine. Don't steal nothing from me. If you need something, ask. I'll try to help out."

As I listened to Anthony, I worked at putting my bunk in order. I had only the few items I'd received at supply—state-issued toothpaste, soap, towels, and three sets of greens, along with underwear and socks—and I stored those in a wooden footlocker at the foot of the bed.

"Make damn sure you keep that locker locked," my bunkmate warned me. "These guys in here will steal anything."

"I'm familiar with the mentality," I said, evoking a smile. Then, as I was about to ask him about retrieving my property from Somers, two young, wisecracking toughs came sauntering up to the bunk.

"Yo. New man in the dorm!" spouted the black kid. "What's up, son?"

"This is your son?" sneered the Latino. Then, in an aside to me, he added, "Yo, man, I think the brother is trying to disrespect you."

"Well, we certainly can't have any of that," I said.

The black kid shot me a look that combined curiosity and restrained anger. "'Well! We certainly can't have any of that!'" he mimicked, then said, "Yo, where you from, mah man?"

"Of late I'm from J-3, thirteen," I replied.

"You was at the prison?" snickered the Latino.

"Four years, brother," I responded with a confident laugh.

"Well, shee, man, you sound like somebody just rolled in from West Hartford," he said, sticking out a hand. "I'm Courage. Courage White. This is my man, Jorge. You got a cigarette, brother?"

"No. Sorry," I told him. "I quit up at the prison."

"Yeah, that's cool," he said. "Lots of bums up there. Hey, you need anything, you just look me up."

"Thanks," I said, as the two kids walked away laughing.

Having silently observed the interaction, Anthony commented, "Brother Courage knows a lot about bums. You'd be wise to steer clear of him. Feelers, that's what I call them. They feel you out to see how you gonna act. You're a little strange, but you done all right."

I was relieved that I'd passed my first test. I knew that the "feelers," as Anthony called them, would be making inquiries with other Somers transplants to find out if I was a gang affiliate, a known informant, a homosexual, or a sex offender, and—very importantly—whether I would stand up for myself in a confrontation. I felt intimidated and ill at ease around most of my inmate peers, but early on I had discovered that I was better off not putting up a front of false machismo. I was certain that I had been kept safe only by prayer and the respect the art had earned me.

"On your bunks for the count! On your bunks for the count!" The words came over the crackling speakers and were followed by a flurry of men moving about and retreating to their respective bunks, accompanied by a lot of clamor and shouting. Then three correctional officers entered the dormitory from the windowed central guard's office, which the inmates referred to as "the Bubble."

"TVs, radios, off!" shouted one of the blue-and-gray-clad guards. "Everybody up on your bunk. Quiet. Quiet." It was nine o'clock.

The C.O.s quickly paced through the dormitory, inspecting the bunks. This was one of four counts that took place every day, and they completed it within five minutes.

"It's lights-out time now, gentlemen," one of them announced. "No more talking. No more visiting."

As I crawled onto my bunk, I saw two inmates scramble for the phone bank, which, like the one at Somers, permitted collect calls only. They picked up and immediately slammed down the receivers—the phones had been turned off. It occurred to me that I should have called Melanie or Pastor Doug to let them know about the transfer, and I kicked myself for not having thought of it sooner.

The following morning I awoke to the soon-to-be-familiar crackle of the dormitory loudspeakers. "Building Six, B side, breakfast in ten minutes! B side, first call for breakfast!" It was a Wednesday, near the end of April 1992. I hadn't previously noticed that there were two sections to the building, each of which was a mirror image of the other. It seemed like a dangerous arrangement, considering that there were only three guards assigned to the unit. But I let the thought pass as I prepared to have my first meal at CRCI. It seemed awfully early. The phones were not yet turned on, and I learned that they wouldn't be until nine o'clock.

"If the pigs feel like turning them on," remarked the disgruntled inmate when I asked about them.

The dormitories were arranged in a C formation, and walkways led from them out to "the Circle." About fifty yards in diameter and bounded by an asphalt walkway, the Circle surrounded a grassy hillock ornamented with shrubs, flower beds, and a flagpole, where the Stars and Stripes flew above the Connecticut state flag. Wooden picnic tables were situated at eight-foot intervals around the circle. It seemed an incongruously attractive arrangement.

I marched with a group of about thirty other early risers around the Circle and to the mess hall. That morning's breakfast consisted of oatmeal, two doughnuts, and coffee. I sat with Anthony, who explained that I would be called to Classification sometime that morning, and that I should start my inquiries about my art supplies there. It sounded like a good plan, and I hoped that I might even see Deputy Warden Belmont.

"One more thing, Ray," Anthony whispered before we returned our metal breakfast trays to the dishwasher window and headed back to the dorm. "Be careful who you talk to and what you say. Whatever you might read in the inmate handbook about chain of command and stuff, the gangs run this place. The Neta, Latin Kings, Twenty-Love, and the Nation are in charge. Just be careful, mah man."

"Yeah," I quietly responded. "I know about the gangs. Hell, I was up at the prison for four years."

"This ain't like the prison, though," he replied. "The prison got cells and separated blocks. Carl Robinson got no containment. This place is an arena, and from what I'm hearing, the gladiators are getting restless. Just be cool."

As I listened to Anthony's advice, I looked around the dining hall. It was easy to spot the gang members, who displayed their colors either on their hats or on pieces of cloth hanging from their back pockets. I suddenly felt uneasy in the CRCI gladiator pit.

"THIS IS WONDERFUL NEWS!" Melanie all but cheered over the telephone later that day, when I was finally able to call her. "You're in a minimum-security facility. It means you're movin' on out. Great!"

She had taken the news about the Board of Pardons rejection in stride, it seemed. Her reaction reassured me of her faith in and commitment to me, but at the same time it angered me. Maybe, it suddenly occurred to me, she had felt certain from the beginning that my request for a pardon would be turned down. Maybe she shared little hope in my dreams after all, I thought, and perhaps she had viewed my attempt to be pardoned as sheer folly. We had been aware all along, I considered, that the Board of Pardons could turn down my application, no matter how much we hoped that they wouldn't. Melanie hadn't let the setback stifle her hope—unless she was really depressed about it and didn't want to share her honest feelings. It was too much for me. "You're not in here, damn it!" I burst out. "I am! I'm never getting out, and you don't care!" I was seething.

"Look, Ray," she said, "your buddy Gino told you from the start that the whole pardons-board thing is little more than a political facade. The fact that all you received in the mail was a brief form letter almost totally verifies that. They probably didn't even look at the package we sent. Now, you can let that piss you off, or you can just go on. There's still a lot of great stuff happening. The transfer to Minimum is one of them. Cheer up."

"Yeah, you're right," I said. "But I still have the problem of not knowing what happened with my art supplies. What if they don't let me have them? Even if they do, I don't know how in hell I'm going to work in this place!"

"It sounds to me like you just want to be upset, and you're going to pull out all the stops to feel that way," she commented. "Get an appointment, or whatever, to see Captain Delmonte."

"Deputy Warden Belmont," I corrected her.

"Whatever," Melanie intoned with growing exasperation. "Get in to see him and talk it over. The artwork is something he'll remember. How can he not?" She concluded, "Listen, you do what you need to do about the art supplies. I've got to get myself and a seven-year-old ready to drive to Connecticut. If you can, call me at Pastor Doug's tonight. Otherwise, I'll see you tomorrow. I love you."

"G'bye," I muttered.

I realized that I was feeling sorry for myself. I didn't often entertain such feelings, but I was sure they were common among prison inmates. I had met plenty who spent most of their time consumed by self-pity. They were miserable, and they counted off their time in agonizing minutes. With a year to wait before the pardons board would meet again, and at least that much time to serve toward my sentence, I couldn't bear the thought of being numbered among those constantly grieving souls. I made up my mind to deal with it.

33. Unadvisable to Complain

"Materson, 162895, report to Substance Abuse Services," blared the dorm P.A. system.

It was early morning, and I had just finished making up my bed. I put down the book I was about to start reading and followed the order.

The SAS office was located near CRCI's front gate, in a wood-frame modular-home unit that looked somewhat out of place among the cinder-block buildings at Carl Robinson. I waited in the lobby for twenty minutes before being called in to see Peter Carver, the SAS program supervisor, who looked to be about my own age.

"Hello, Ray," he said.

"Good morning," I greeted him in return.

"I'm going to cut to the chase here," he said as he perused a file he held in his hands. "We're in the process of starting a residential drug-and-alcohol treatment facility at Carl Robinson. It's a new, innovative program for inmates with a history of substance-abuse problems. The plan calls for sixty participants who will all live in the same dorm. These inmates will attend drug-education classes and be required to attend AA and NA meetings at least twice a week. It's for inmates who are motivated to change their lives and work toward recovery as a long-term goal. Your name was given to Deputy Warden Belmont. He said you might be interested in being part of it."

I didn't need to hear any more of his pitch. This was a gift. "Where do I sign up?" I asked.

"Now, that's the kind of enthusiasm I like to see," he said with a smile. "I'll give you our information package. It includes the rules of the program and a personal-history questionnaire for you to fill out. We hope to start moving inmates into the dorm in about a week. Any questions?"

"Sounds like a good program, Mr. Carver," I said. "I do have a question: I just got moved here, and I'm wondering when I might get my property back from the prison."

The smile evaporated from his face. "We don't have anything to do with transfers of property," he said curtly. "I meant, Do you have any questions about the program."

"No, I guess not," I said. "Not right now."

"Okay, then fill out the history and return it to your dorm officer. Bye."

He dismissed me summarily.

I began to feel that things might be working out. Sustaining one's emotional stability in prison is not an easy task. It's like walking a tightrope. It was no easier for Melanie. She had no outlet for her feelings, whether sorrow, disappointment, or anger, as she had to bolster my crumbling control. This was yet another test, the one that causes the crack-up of most domestic relationships. The prison system chews families up and spits them out. While politicians simultaneously try to straddle the platforms of "supporting family values" and "being tough on crime," we were balanced precariously on a taut wire, trying not to fall into the gears of the machine.

The visiting room at CRCI was far different from the one at Somers. Instead of long rows of tables, it had cushioned seats arranged like those in the waiting area of an airport or train station. The walls were painted white and blue-gray, except for the rear wall, which was almost entirely glass, allowing for ample sunlight. At the front of the expansive room was a long desk, where the guards sat and scrutinized the interactions between inmates and their visitors. That's where I met Melanie as she entered the room and handed her pass to the desk officer.

The female guard smiled at us and said, "Sit wherever you like."

I took Melanie's hand, and we took two adjoining seats near a side wall.

"Wow, look at this place!" she said with a sparkling smile.

I leaned over and kissed her, then asked how everything was going.

"Oh, we're fine," she said. "How's about you? Tell me about the new digs."

I told her about my meeting with Pete Carver and about the treatment program. I told her that I was still unable to find out anything about when—or even if—my art supplies would be returned to me.

"Give it a little time," she advised, poking me lightly in the ribs. "Hey, look! I can touch you!"

We spent our hour together simply enjoying each other's presence and stealing kisses. It was the first time in our odd courtship that we had been able to sit beside each other or have any physical contact beyond holding hands across a table, and the experience was as exciting as it was frustrating. Longing to be closer and to share the intimacy that privacy affords, we felt as though we had been time-warped back to some Victorian-era parlor. The situation was laughable, but it also had a pure, spiritual element that we recognized and appreciated.

The guard approached to tell us that our time was up. We stood up in a single motion. Looking into Melanie's eyes, I spoke to her in exaggerated stage English: " 'I burn, I pine, I perish!' "

"*Romeo and Juliet*?" she guessed.

"*Shrew*," I corrected her.

"I don't like the implication, sir," she intoned, stepping away in a mock flurry. Then she added, "I'll see you tomorrow."

Having to do without my art supplies remained a distressing situation for me. I felt as though I were missing a limb. Over the past three years, not a day had gone by that I hadn't invested at least a little time in my creative pursuits. I had spent eight to ten hours embroidering on most of those days. Time seemed to pass fleetingly when I was lost in the little world bounded by my sewing hoop.

It took several inmate-request forms and a meeting with Pete Carver and Deputy Warden Belmont for me to recover my sewing supplies. I had been at CRCI for a month by the time I was finally called down to Property to pick them up. I witnessed a cursory inspection of my supplies by one Officer Vega. He rummaged through the bag, glancing at each item, and he threw some of them into a trash can instead of giving them to me. When I asked him why I couldn't have an extra Rubbermaid bowl, he said, "Oh, you could probably have this, Materson, but I don't like you, so I'm throwing it away."

In the end, Mr. Vega handed me a large cardboard box that contained about two-thirds of the socks and other items I'd collected at Somers for my embroidery work. By order of the warden, he was supposed to remove only those items that were specifically designated as "contraband unrelated to art supplies." But at Carl Robinson, even orders from the warden weren't always followed. The guards had ways of evening scores with any inmates who happened to incur their anger or hostility, and they could make life very unpleasant for any of us, so I knew it was unadvisable to complain. Instead, I thanked him when he handed me the box containing what remained of my supplies, and I returned to the dorm.

• • •

34. Time

By the time I got my art supplies back it was May, and the days were getting longer with the approach of summer. I had been moved from Building Six's B side to its A side, which had been designated to house inmates enrolled in the drug-treatment program, known as TIME, an acronym for This I Must Earn. Pete Carver seemed highly dedicated to the project. He regularly visited the program's sixty or so inmates to give pep talks. He applauded our efforts when he found them praiseworthy and admonished inmates who missed group meetings.

For a prison situation, the TIME program dorm was reasonably safe turf. There were few fights, and those of us who genuinely wanted to better ourselves worked to make life in the unit a positive experience. The best testament to our success, it turned out, was a by-product of a negative chain of events that unfolded at Carl Robinson on a rainy day in June. A fight among rival gangs erupted into a full-scale riot throughout the compound, and for several hours, swarms of inmates ran rampant from one end of the place to the other. Numerous guards and dozens of inmates were injured, windows and furnishings were broken, and several fires were started. By the time the Corrections Emergency Response Team and state troopers brought the situation under control, tens of thousands of dollars' worth of damage had been done to all of the dormitories except one: Building Six, Side A. Press accounts of the riot failed to credit the TIME program inmates for keeping the peace amid the chaos, but it was clear that Pete Carver was proud of us. We—or at least most of us—were simply relieved and thankful.

The move to CRCI and my involvement with the TIME program changed my art-making routine significantly. I could no longer remain on my bunk for hours at a time, working on my creations, because I was assigned a job as a yardman. This meant that on weekdays at 7:00 A.M. I reported to the groundskeepers' building where I was issued a broom and a plastic bag and sent out on the compound to sweep and pick up trash. I was one of forty or fifty inmates who had such assignments, which earned us fifteen dollars a month.

My art-making sessions were further limited by TIME program classes—largely informational group sessions that dealt with issues ranging from cultural awareness to self-esteem building and the dangers of drug abuse. These meetings generally lasted an hour, and they were always facilitated by counselors from the drug-treatment office, sometimes accompanied by a corrections guard. On the whole, these gatherings generated a lot of genuine interest and active participation, but they were often started with the playing of simple games or brainteaser exercises, and some of the inmates found such activities annoying. They gave me an idea, though.

As a college student, I'd spent a great deal of time studying improvisational theater, and much of that work had involved storytelling and playing games. Why not, I thought, get a few motivated inmates together and start our own improvisational theater group? It took some doing, including preparation of a formal proposal and several meetings with Pete Carver and other officials, but by the fall of 1992 I'd received the necessary permission. Almost immediately, I began meeting twice a week with ten or twelve other inmates in a large conference room, where we played, shared life experiences, and developed scripts.

I soon noticed that playing simple, noncompetitive games tended to break down barriers and stimulate positive interaction among the group's members. We were convicted criminals —thieves from the streets, muggers, and drug dealers, from a variety of backgrounds and circumstances that might seem strange and in some cases frightening. And yet there we were, laughing together over a game of Duck, Duck, Goose like a bunch of happy children.

It was shortly after the theater group became active that I came to know Hugo M. Almost twenty years my senior, he was a member of Alcoholics Anonymous, and he was one of several volunteers from the surrounding communities who would hold weekly AA meetings at Carl Robinson. The first time I heard Hugo speak at one of these meetings, I was deeply moved at the way he bravely shared the story of the tragedies and humiliations he had known in his life.

I recognized that my artwork had been a major factor in my recovery from my addictions, but the TIME program, my involvement with AA, and the impending production of an anti-drug poster featuring my design helped me fully appreciate the need for my continued sobriety. It was at least partly in recognition of that need—and largely with Melanie's encouragement —that I began creating more works with autobiographical themes. That helped remind me of what my life had been like before addiction, and of the depths to which I had sunk when in its grip.

During a visit that Melanie made to CRCI in October, there was plenty of business for us to discuss. "Next week you'll be getting a visit from Sam Connor, who's with the Connecticut Prison Association," she told me. "He's going to be bringing some people from Aetna Insurance to photograph you and get some more information for the poster. Whitey Jenkins, who's a curator for the Aetna Art Gallery, will be with them. You'll like Whitey. He helped get this whole ball rolling."

"This is great, Mel. Are you going to be with them?" I asked.

"I'm going to try to make it, but it's a long drive, and I also have an appointment to meet with one of the curators at the Museum of American Folk Art in the city." She beamed as she told me this.

"What city?" I asked.

"*The city,*" she said with extra emphasis. "New York."

"This is pretty important, I take it," I responded flatly.

"Ray, it's New York, the art capital of the world!" she exclaimed, now animated. "You need to know this stuff! New York is the venue that either makes you or breaks you. It's the Big Apple, Ray."

The prospect of having my work recognized in New York

seemed light years from bartering little Puerto Rican flags for cigarettes. Still, I was intimidated by my surroundings, which told me I didn't yet deserve to feel too good about myself. A glance at my prison garb reinforced that unpleasant feeling. Looking around the visiting room and observing the misery and hopelessness on the faces of my peers, I felt, in that moment, a deep sense of compassion for the same men who often frightened and perplexed me. I realized, too, that although I looked like everyone else, I ultimately perceived myself as an observer.

"Where did you go?" Melanie asked as I emerged from my brief reverie and made eye contact with her again.

"I don't think I know." I said. "I'm really happy, though. Thanks for all your hard work. I sure hope it pays off for you."

"For us, Ray," she said. "For us."

35. A New York Connection

On the Tuesday following my discussion with Melanie about the poster and her plans for taking my work to New York, I was called to the administration building's front offices. At the deputy warden's office I was met and greeted by a small entourage. Warden Belmont and Pete Carver were all smiles and handshakes, and one of the secretaries even offered me a cup of coffee. Clad in my prison greens among these people in business clothes, I revisited my self-negating feelings of the previous week. Everyone treated me as if I were someone very special.

After introductions all around, Sam Connor and Whitey

Jenkins explained the poster project, and a woman representing Aetna Insurance asked me to sign a contract. "It's really more of a release form," she explained, "stating that you give us permission to photograph you and your work for purposes of promoting the poster."

Then I was taken outside for a photo shoot. The photographer, a pleasant man in a tan suit, had me pose next to fences and coils of razor wire. Turning me this way and that way, he tried to capture my face in sunlight, then posed me more in shadow. He photographed me smiling and not smiling. I felt like an object, a temporarily high-priced item in a warehouse of social rejects.

After the brief contract-signing ceremony, Melanie had been hustled out of the facility, but she watched from the other side of the fence as I was photographed. She sat on the hood of her car and waved and nodded encouragingly from the prison parking lot. Because she had marshaled the forces to make the poster a reality, I knew that the moment was as much hers as it was mine, and I wanted to be with her. I framed a picture in my mind of the two of us looking through the fence at each other. My heart stung as I considered the circumstances of our love, and at that moment a jet from a nearby air force base thundered over like a bird of prey.

Soon the moment vanished. The camera was put away, and parting handshakes were swiftly exchanged. Warden Belmont approached me and whispered with assurance that he'd sent for a lunch, since I'd missed the noon chow call. In the triumph of the moment, I expected something more extravagant than the usual prison fare. Five minutes later, another green-clad inmate strode up to me and handed me a brown paper bag.

"Bologna and cheese," he said with a distracted grin. "Think I could have the orange?"

I gave it to him as we walked back to our dormitories.

Melanie, who had grown more comfortable staying overnight with Pastor Doug and his wife, returned that evening. She had felt largely left out during the poster meeting and was upset over being shut out of the compound before the photo shoot. "But I'll get over it," she said. "Besides, we've got bigger projects on the horizon. I didn't have a chance to tell you this morning, but I made the trip to the city yesterday. It was pretty thrilling for a girl who used to call it home turf."

"How did that go?" I asked.

"Well, I'll give you the bad news first," she began. "The people at the folk art museum liked your work, but they felt that you weren't, how shall I say, 'folksy' enough for their venue. You've got a college degree and—"

"And what," I began. "I'm too sophisticated? Heck, I'm 'bout as *ignerent* as they come . . . just set me on a porch with a little banjo music in the background . . ."

Melanie chuckled. "Actually they were very pleasant," she said. "You'll see when you meet them one day."

"So what's the good news?" I asked.

"Well, I wanted to make the most of my trip," she continued

with growing excitement, "soooo, in the lobby I started looking through a copy of a folk art magazine, and then I started making phone calls to some of the galleries that were advertised in it. Well, since it was Monday, a lot of them were closed, but the first one I found open, American Primitive, told me to stop by."

"Cool," I said.

"You don't know how cool," she replied. " I sashayed over to the gallery—you'll like this—on Broadway, and the curator and his wife were floored. I mean, the owner practically drooled! So you're in! He's putting some of your work in his next group exhibit."

"Well, this is good news," I said.

"Ray, it's not just good news. It's great news," she said. "There are thousands of artists in New York dying to get gallery representation. Lifetimes are spent trying to get into shows, and you made it on the first try!"

"Well, we have the poster project going and a gallery in the city. Now what?" I asked.

"Now you've got to keep turning out artwork, Ray," Melanie replied without skipping a beat.

It was a lot to take in.

"You did a Babe Ruth piece recently," she reminded me. "The curator at American Primitive was especially impressed by it, and so was I. Everybody *loves baseball,* Ray, everybody—meaning not only art collectors but judges, prosecuting attorneys, and Board of Pardons members. It's all that stuff James Earl Jones said in *Field of Dreams,* about baseball being a part

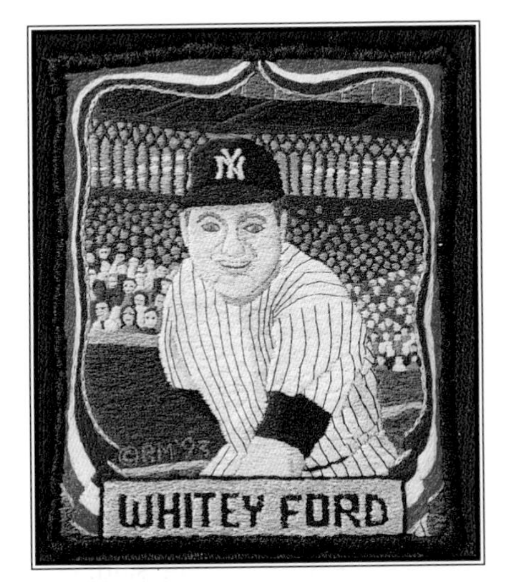
WHITEY FORD
©RM'93

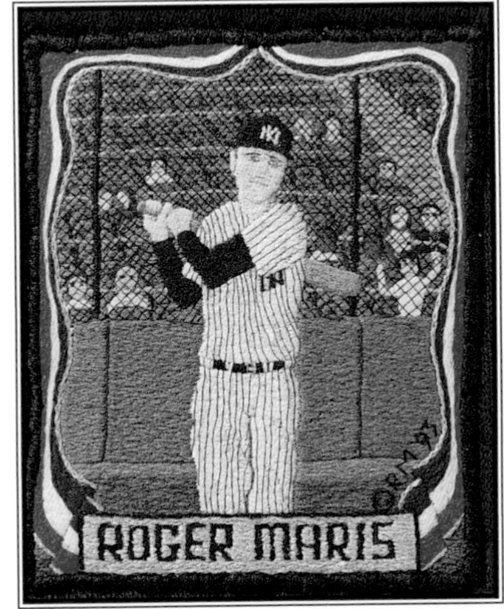
ROGER MARIS

JOE JACKSON
©RM'95

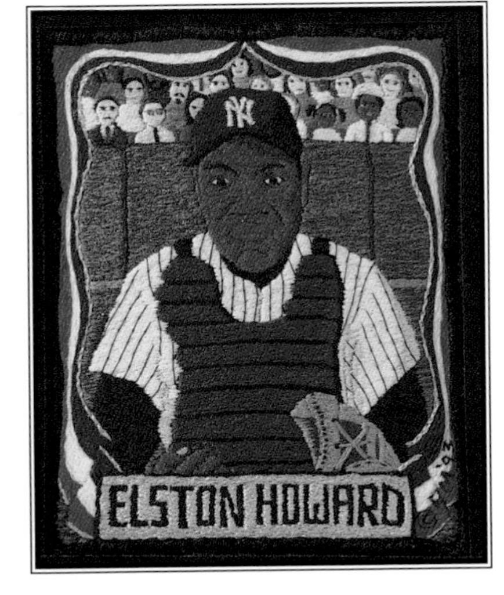
ELSTON HOWARD

of our culture and heritage. It's family picnics, the sights and sounds of the ballpark. Baseball, Ray. Think about it."

"Time's up, folks," announced the visiting-room guard as he unexpectedly approached us.

We kissed and parted ways in the visiting room.

Back on my bunk, I considered Melanie's suggestion. I remembered the fields of my youth and the joy I'd felt in looking through stacks of baseball cards. I recalled brushing the faint powder residue from the faces of my heroes, left from the sticks of bubble gum that were in the packages, and savoring the smell. I often fell asleep clutching the entire Yankee lineup in my small hand.

36. The Honeymoon

As Christmas approached, there were several announcements of good news from Melanie and from my new art dealer, Aarne Anton at American Primitive. During the first week of the show in New York, three of my pieces sold, and within a few more weeks the inventory Melanie had left at the gallery was almost completely sold out. My miniature embroideries had become successful commodities almost overnight, and it was hard not to be overjoyed. I called Pastor Doug and asked him to come visit me, because I had something important to discuss with him.

"We like Melanie and John a great deal, Ray," said the clergyman when I told him what was on my mind. "But this is a very big step."

"I love her, Doug," I said again. "I want to marry her."

Aarne Anton happily accepted my frequent phone calls from the prison, and he agreed to send the check for my next art sale to Pastor Doug. It was a slightly awkward arrangement, but Doug had told me that he and Leanne knew of a lovely little jewelry store, where they'd done business in the past. They were as excited as I was as the plan unfolded.

A few days before Christmas, I sat alongside Melanie in the CRCI visiting room. I kept losing the thread of our conversation and looking past her at the entrance to the large room.

"What's wrong with you today?" Melanie asked.

"Oh, nothing," I said, making a lame gesture toward a corrections officer. "That guard's a punk."

Surprised to hear a remark that she rightly considered very much out of character, she echoed, "What guard is a 'punk'?"

At that moment, Pastor Doug walked into the room with a spring in his step. Approaching us, he handed me a small box and smiled broadly as he said, "Special delivery."

On cue, I got down on one knee and opened the box, offering the ring inside it to Melanie as I asked her if she would marry me. All eyes in the waiting room seemed to suddenly focus in our direction.

"Of course, I'll marry you, Mr. Materson," Melanie said with tears in her eyes.

"Kiss her already," one of the guards murmured.

So I did.

It was four months later—on a gloriously sunny day—that we gathered in a large conference room to take our wedding vows. Melanie looked beautiful in a white vintage suit and matching hat. Joey Paca—my connection at Carl Robinson through my old friend Gino—worked in inmate clothing, and he had hooked me up with a new set of greens. Accompanied by his wife, Leanne, Pastor Doug was, of course, there to perform the ceremony. Also on hand were Pete Carver, Deputy Warden Belmont, Whitey Jenkins, Sam Connor, and a bright but fidgety curator from an art gallery in Hartford. Melanie's son, John, by this time eight years old, was our ring bearer. I had met him only on one previous occasion, which Melanie had characterized as "the John test," referring—or so I'd assumed—to the old premise that children and dogs can instinctively gauge a person's character and true intentions. Despite the surroundings and my prison garb, I had evidently passed.

A few minutes before the ceremony, a woman approached me and began asking questions about my art, the length of my sentence, the circumstances of the crime I had committed, and my relationship with Melanie. It all seemed slightly incongruous with what was about to take place, and I didn't understand what was going on until Melanie explained that the woman was a reporter for the *Manchester Journal Inquirer*—a fact that I had been too distracted to catch if the woman had mentioned it when she'd introduced herself.

"Hey," Melanie whispered to me in an aside, "it ain't the *New York Times*. But the press is something you need to get used to."

And so it was that we were married. The ceremony and "reception" lasted an hour or so; then I was ushered back to Building Six, where I had to await being summoned again for the walk to the honeymoon trailer. Conjugal visits at CRCI didn't typically take place until thirty days after an inmate's wedding —a regulation established presumably to allow the bride time to entertain any second thoughts, so that she could decide to back out before the marriage was consummated. However, in no small part due to Joey Paca's lobbying the powers that be regarding my "celebrity" status, the usual waiting period had been waived in my case. It was all rather remarkable, and it turned out to be a foretaste of other extraordinary events that would follow in the coming months.

In a breach of my usual habits, I watched the minutes tick by on the large, black-numeraled clock in the dormitory. As the hands met on the 12, the dormitory speakers crackled with the terse call, "Materson, trailer visit."

Grabbing the paper bag in which I'd packed my provisions for the twenty-four-hour honeymoon—toothbrush, flip-flop sandals, and a change of underwear—I was led to the trailer by a corrections officer.

The honeymoon trailer was a large, rather dated mobile-home unit just inside the fence on the east side of CRCI, near a secondary entrance to the facility. It was also enclosed within its own fence, surmounted by the familiarly menacing coils of razor wire. On another occasion, I might have been amused or appalled by the absurdity of such a scene—being led out to mate in a cage —but there was a strange charm and a feeling of predestination in knowing that I was finally going to be alone with the woman I loved. The bizarre surroundings and circumstances be damned, I thought.

The C.O. walked me up the steps to the trailer's main door and instructed me to sit down in the dingy kitchen area while he conducted a brief inspection of the premises. "It ain't no Holiday Inn, Mattie," he said. Then, in a last, handicapped effort at amusement, he added, "Don't do anything I wouldn't do."

Closing the door behind him, he left me sitting alone at the table. Outside I could hear Melanie's voice and that of another C.O. The door opened again, and there stood Melanie, holding a large suitcase and a grocery bag. I quickly got up and took them from her, placing them just out of the way before I picked her up in both my arms and carried her across the threshold, then set her down on the battered sofa. The C.O. who followed her in was also carrying a couple of bags, and he set them down, then turned to walk out.

"You'll be eating good tonight," he said. "Don't forget to call in at three and nine for the counts," he added, pointing to a telephone on the kitchen counter. "We'll be up to get you at ten tomorrow morning. Have a good time, and congratulations."

As the door closed, Melanie and I nervously looked at each other. Our relationship had been a deep but celibate friendship for more than two years, with sexual feelings and the need for physical intimacy pushed into the background. Neither of us said much for several minutes, while I helped Melanie unpack the supplies she had brought. There were two thick-cut steaks, potatoes, salad fixings, bread, soda, snacks, a cake, and ice cream. We laughed at how much food she had packed.

"They wouldn't let me bring in the sparkling grape juice," she said, sounding annoyed and a little sad.

"Hey," I replied, "as long as you're here, it doesn't matter." We kissed, softly at first, then more deeply.

"Honey," she whispered as she gently pushed me away, "I'm anxious, too. But I'm not ready yet. Besides," she laughed, "we've still got some unpacking to do."

I was actually somewhat relieved by her seeming timidity. There was much to be savored in the moment, and I wanted to take in every second of it—to taste it, revel in it, and live it out between ticks of the clock.

"Go make the bed," she said, handing me a new set of sheets.

Like the rest of the trailer's interior, the master bedroom walls were lined with dark, fake-wood paneling. The room was furnished only with a queen-sized bed, a cheap clock radio, and a set of empty, built-in cabinets. The window was covered with drapes that looked as if they'd been salvaged from a trash heap, and there were no pictures or other decorations. As I made the bed and fluffed the pillows Melanie had brought, I considered all the effort she had made in preparation for this day, and I was overcome with a sudden feeling of sadness. A new bride, I thought, should have so much more than I could offer—a drab, cheerless room in a trailer surrounded by razor wire on the grounds of a state prison. I felt a tear form in the corner of my eye.

"This place could use a little brightening up," Melanie remarked, entering the room with a softly flickering candle in her hand.

The candlelight enhanced the natural glow of her beautiful

face. She smiled, and in an instant the gloomy feeling that had taken hold of me vanished. She set down the candle in its holder, and the sound of distant thunder moved us close together. As raindrops began to patter on the metal roof, we melted into each other's arms and slowly dropped down onto the bed. We held each other and giggled quietly as we rolled across the fresh-smelling blankets. Overcome by love and mutual desire, accompanied by the sounds of thunder and rain, and knowing that our time together would be all too brief, we consummated our vows of love in that strange setting.

Throughout the afternoon and into the evening we loved, talked, laughed, and snacked. Then Melanie prepared the steaks and trimmings she had brought, and we enjoyed a candlelight dinner. The sound of the scratchy clock radio harmonized with the waves of thundershowers that continued to blow through the area well into the evening.

"You know," Melanie said, "this whole thing just gets more country-and-western every minute!"

"What do you mean?" I asked, savoring a mouthful of béarnaise-drenched asparagus.

"Well, look at this place." She gestured at our surroundings. "It's like some fishing cabin or prospector's camp out in the woods." Then she broke into an improvised version of an old David Allan Coe song about marrying in prison with only "one night for makin' love."

I joined in for the chorus.

"God, I love you," I said, giggling.

"After tonight I don't know how I'm going to live without you by me all the time," Melanie said.

37. TEAM PORTRAIT

I didn't know how I was going to live without Melanie, either. Our twenty-four-hour honeymoon had been a beautiful, delicious tease that was gone like a wisp of vapor. Such conjugal visits were allowed only once every six weeks or so, and there was persistent talk of the possibility that the state might end the practice entirely. I tried to ignore this dire forecast, but it wasn't easy.

Still, I stayed busy. I continued to attend TIME program meetings, and I kept the momentum going with the theater project, which was taxing work, both physically and emotionally. As always, though, it was the artwork that grounded me. At Melanie's suggestion, I began a series of portraits to personally immortalize my baseball heroes from years past—the 1963 New York Yankees.

By the end of August I was completing both my substance-abuse treatment and the last two Yankees portraits—Roger Maris and Whitey Ford. Pete Carver had asked me to remain involved in the TIME program as a mentor for newly enrolled inmates—an agreeable prospect, in my mind. And Aarne Anton was evidently thrilled with the growing group of baseball images, which he was saving to sell as a set when it was complete.

Baseball figured prominently in another aspect of my life, too. The Building Six softball team, composed largely of Puerto Rican and Dominican gang members, had established a winning record on the compound as well as among neighboring prison teams. The team served as a strong symbol of what can be accomplished through sobriety and willingness to work together. Its members contributed to a sense of unity in the dorm, and we were all proud of their unprecedented record of victories.

I was particularly moved the evening the team paraded into the dormitory after winning the regional prison softball championship. The men's jerseys were merely T-shirts with numerals drawn on them with felt-tip pens, and their green prison pants wore the dirt and stains of a tough game. The baseball mitts that they joyously tossed in the air looked as though they'd been around since Babe Ruth's day. But they were the champions! The cheers, chants, hugs, and jibes that they shared were pure, transcending the shame, guilt, and coarse mediocrity of their uniforms and surroundings. It wasn't a program of recovery that brought the entire dorm into a state of united single-mindedness. It was something as simple as a baseball game.

Inspired by the occasion, I wrote a letter to the deputy warden in charge of treatment and programs, explaining that I felt this sort of experience should somehow be remembered and rewarded. "These men," I wrote, "will never have high-school or college yearbook photos to look back on with pride. Do you think a group picture could be taken, so that they will at least have this moment to savor for a lifetime? It was a good, honest moment, one which says that teamwork and living clean has inherent rewards." I was very hopeful.

A week later, I received a written response: "Dear Mr. Materson: Group photographs of prison inmates are not permitted at CRCI. Very truly yours, Deputy Warden Smythe."

My anger at the refusal of my request was only heightened by the terseness of the message. It seemed to me that the idea of a group photograph was entirely consistent with everything that "treatment" and "rehabilitation" were supposed to be about. Because I had told a number of the team members about the letter I'd written, I didn't look forward to informing them that my suggestion had been turned down. I didn't know how they would take the news. As it turned out, a few were angry, but the others seemed more hurt and disappointed, like kids who are told that there's no money to buy anything from the ice-cream vendor. This reaction prompted me to repeat my request and, this time, to include an added incentive.

My work had been consistently selling well, so I wrote back to Deputy Warden Smythe and informed her that if she would permit a group photo of the team to be made, I would recreate it in thread. My own embroidered miniature group portrait, I explained, would then be sent to my gallery in New York, to be exhibited and presumably sold. I told her that I would happily donate a portion of the profits to the Corrections Officers' Benevolent Fund.

That was all it took. I was contacted by the CRCI recreation director, Mr. Harkness, by the end of the following week; he told me that he'd been authorized to take a group photo of the Building Six softball team. In a society that sees few winning seasons, it was an important victory.

Following up on my successful push to get the team photo approved, I distributed copies of the finished photograph to each team member, and when I had completed my embroidered miniature version of it, I arranged to have my piece photographed and gave a copy of that photo to each team member as well. The whole sequence of events amounted to a real per-

sonal triumph for me, but, largely because a few of the team members had been involved with gangs, it was soon to pay off in another way, too.

B. J. HORTON WAS A FELLOW INMATE whom I'd befriended in the TIME program. A carpenter and construction worker before he'd been sent to prison, he was a large man, perhaps a few years my junior, and he walked the compound with little concern about being intimidated or threatened by other inmates. Diplomatic and quite intelligent, he had a sincere smile and a hearty laugh that could fill a room. But B.J. also had a problem that I was unaware of.

I don't know if it was my eternal naïveté or an unconscious refusal to see the evidence of his affliction. In any case, I was clueless when I approached B.J. one afternoon as he sat on his bunk, his head in his hands. He looked as though he'd been crying.

"Hey, Beej, what's going on?" I asked.

He didn't look at me as he responded, "You really don't want to know, Ray."

"Sure I do," I insisted. "What do you think all this recovery stuff is about? If you've got a problem, you should share it. Talk to somebody before it gets the better of you."

Finally meeting my gaze, he said, "You want me to tell you about recovery?" Then, in a quick motion, he pulled his shirt sleeve up to his left biceps and revealed a line of small bruises—tracks, the signature of an active junkie.

"Oh, Jesus, B.J.! What the hell are you doing to yourself?" I asked softly.

"I'm 'in the life' again, Ray, boy." He grinned falsely.

"But you're in the program," I started to argue. "I thought you . . ."

"Well, you thought wrong," he said, cutting me off. "I hate to tell you this, but I've been using the whole time I've been in this messed-up program. I can't kick. Hell, I don't want to kick. I can't imagine walking around this place straight, with all the jerks and knuckleheads to deal with."

"So I guess you think I'm a jerk and a knucklehead, too," I said, genuinely a little hurt and angry at his comment.

"C'mon, man," he said, "I don't mean you. I just mean . . . Oh, hell, what's the use. I'm in trouble. Big trouble."

"Well, maybe I can help," I offered.

"No," B.J. said, composing himself. "I don't think so, buddy."

"Try me," I persisted.

"You can't tell anybody," he said in a near whisper, "but I'm into the gangs for three hundred and fifty bucks."

Money and drugs are very serious business in the prison system, in perhaps an even more heinous way than they are on the street. It surprised me that B.J. had let himself get so deeply in debt, because I'd been given to understand that lines of credit rarely went beyond one hundred dollars. In any case, I knew very well that paying off his debt could be a mortal ordeal.

"Ray, these guys own me," he told me. "I'm gonna get hurt."

Lines of fear and worry seemed to sprout on B.J.'s face like vines on a trellis. "They own me, Ray," he repeated.

I was sure of that, too, and I felt obliged to help. My efforts toward getting the group baseball-team photo had promoted good relations with those team members who were also friends of members of the Latin Kings, and I thought they might be receptive to my assistance with this critical matter, as long as it produced the result they wanted.

"Listen, B.J.," I said. "I'm pulling down some pretty good money selling art in New York. What if I paid your debt for you?"

"No, man," he quickly responded, "I couldn't let you do that."

"Why not?" I asked.

"The truth?" he replied. "Because if you take care of this bill for me, I'll just run it up again. I'm a freaking dirtbag, Ray—a stone junkie and a loser." Then he said, "Thanks anyway," and walked slowly away.

B.J.'s self-deprecating honesty hit me hard. I liked him, and I believed he was capable of making a life for himself if he could overcome his addiction. But I knew the drug debt could literally do him in. With or without his blessing, I felt compelled to act.

The following afternoon, during recreation out on the circle, I approached Julio, a softball-team player who I knew was a member of the Kings, posted to observe the interactions of everyone within his eyesight on the compound. This was standard procedure for the prison gangs. If trouble or anything unusual started taking place, the "guard posts" would alert higher-ups in the chains of command. The lieutenants and vice presidents typically held court over games of cards or dominoes at the picnic tables. About two-thirds of the 750 inmates at CRCI were gang members, so when trouble erupted, it often meant trouble for everyone.

Julio was a tall, thin Puerto Rican with freckles that were barely discernible on his brown skin. When he saw me, he gave only a brief nod.

"Hey, Julio, what's happening?" I asked.

"Not too much," he responded, maintaining his attentive guard-post posture.

It was an extremely delicate situation, so I spoke as softly and discreetly as I could: "Julio, I need to talk to somebody about someone who might be having some problems."

Sensing the urgency of the matter, he focused more closely on me, asking, "What is the trouble?"

"Well, this person I know . . ." I hesitated. "Well, he might owe some money to some people for a bad habit he has."

"So what?" he said. "Everybody got money problems."

"Well," I responded, "I might know somebody who would like to help him out."

Julio gave me a severe look and, without saying anything else, walked over to one of the picnic tables. I tried not to be too obvious as I watched him lean into a group of Latinos who were playing dominoes and talking animatedly. When Julio started talking, the table fell still and silent, and in a moment the whole group, along with others who had been sitting at an adjoining table, headed in my direction. I soon found myself enclosed within a tight ring of gang members and their leaders. Julio and a gang leader named Donny each took an extra step or two into the circle and confronted me.

"Donny wants to know who this 'somebody' you know is," Julio said.

"Well, you know how it is," I said, well aware of the unwritten prison rule against speaking too directly about certain sensitive subjects. "He's a white guy in Building Six."

As Julio translated what I had said into Spanish, the eyes of everyone in the circle were glued to Donny, as if awaiting a signal.

Then Julio turned back to me and asked, "It's you that wants to pay this bill?"

"Yes," I said, feeling very nervous. "I just want to help a friend."

Once again, Julio translated my words, and for the first time, Donny looked straight into my eyes and walked up to within a few inches of me. Then he spoke in very broken English.

"You are very good to help a friend," he commended me, "but this is not for you to do. You are a good man. We like you. But this is not something for you to do." As if in a scene in a *Godfather* movie, Donny put his hands on my arms and placed first one cheek, then the other, on either side of my face. "You are a good man," he said again. "Take care of your family."

With that, the circle of men dispersed, and I was left alone to contemplate my stupidity in trying to meddle and my good fortune to have come through the situation not only unscathed but with a new level of respect among at least one large segment of the prison population. The angels had apparently encircled me even more tightly than the Kings.

Two days later, B. J. Horton checked into protective custody, and about a week after that—so I heard—he was transferred to another prison downstate. It was a move I knew wouldn't save him.

For the remainder of my stay at CRCI, Donny never missed an opportunity to greet me when he saw me walking across the grounds. It became something of a regular ceremony for him to take my arms and, with his lieutenants surrounding us, ask me how my family was doing. I invariably told him they were fine, and this always seemed to bring him great delight.

38. THE WALL

In October I received word that the Board of Pardons wouldn't be reviewing my case at their next meeting. The letdown wasn't as severe as it had been for me after they'd rejected my first application, even though Melanie and I had both waited for the decision with considerable optimism this time. We'd solicited more letters of support, and we'd even hired an attorney, but it was all for naught.

Meanwhile, I was working at full bore on my embroidery. With a growing collection of my pieces on hand, Aarne decided to give me a solo exhibition at American Primitive. Working day and night to make as many new pieces as I could for the show, I had little time to mourn my fate. Because of a new rule that prohibited inmates from staying on their bunks during the day, I often worked in the inmate clothing building. Although Joey Paca had been released on parole, he'd introduced me to his connections there, and the C.O. responsible for that area allowed me to use an otherwise vacant office as my studio.

Melanie stayed busy, too, writing press releases and corresponding with Aarne about the exhibit, which was scheduled for December. Every time I saw her or spoke with her on the phone, she had news. The excitement peaked when, one day late in the year, she told me about a major publicity coup.

"*Sports Illustrated*!" she almost shouted into the phone.

"You're kidding!" I said.

"No!" she went on. "I got a call from the gallery today, and Aarne told me that one of their writers had been through the gallery and loved your Yankee series. Anyway, she's going to be contacting Warden Belmont about arranging an interview."

"When?" I asked.

"It sounds as though it's going to be very soon," she said. "Ray, this is absolutely marvelous. *Sports Illustrated!* I mean, it isn't an art magazine, for sure, but it's got a huge circulation."

It was thrilling news, indeed. And Warden Belmont seemed to be as thrilled as we were about it. Two days later, he made a personal appearance at Building Six with a captain and two C.O.s in tow. When he summoned me to the Bubble, he wore a big smile that belied his reputation as a stern administrator.

"Ray," he began, as the heavy steel door into the guard

station was opened for us, "I've got some pretty amazing news for you."

"No, Mattie," Captain Diecklemann jokingly interrupted, "you're not being released."

"I got a call yesterday from a writer for *Sports Illustrated,*" Warden Belmont continued. "She wants to come interview you on Thursday. She saw your artwork down in New York. Congratulations," he concluded, giving me a warm, brisk handshake. Then he asked me to take a walk with him. We left the dormitory and strolled the prison grounds for twenty minutes, during which he talked about his own passion for sports, recounted stories of his days playing college baseball, and rhapsodized about his favorite ball club, the Boston Red Sox. Then he changed the subject abruptly.

"So, I was thinking, Ray," he asked, "how would you feel about painting a mural?"

I knew nothing, of course, about painting murals. I wasn't a painter. "What would the subject be?" I asked.

"Fenway Park!" he replied with a huge grin. "There's a wall outside my office that's just begging to have something painted on it. So, what do you think?"

I could have simply told him that I didn't know how to paint a mural—that I'd never painted much of anything, except houses, during a summer job when I was a college student. But he was the warden. So, I grinned right back at him. "When do I start?" I asked.

"I'd like you to start as soon as possible," he told me.

"But I-I've got this show in New York," I stammered.

"Well, of course you do," he replied. "Plus you'll need to study the pictures I've got and we'll need to order paints for you. So it'll take a little time. You just let me know what you need and when you want to get started."

"Yes, sir," I said. Then we shook hands, and he congratulated me again as we parted company just outside the Bubble.

A week later, only a few days before Christmas, I told Melanie about the mural commission from the warden. She was elated. She had stayed overnight with me in the poorly heated trailer, and we were shivering as we made love and discussed plans for our future.

"This is a great opportunity for you, Ray!" she said.

"Frankly," I told her, "I see it more as an obligation than a 'great opportunity.' "

"You're not seeing the whole picture," she said, "if you'll excuse the pun."

"And what, pray tell, is that?" I asked as we snuggled under the blankets of the well-worn bed.

"Look," she explained, "you'll be out in the front office. You'll be there six, eight hours a day, maybe. Belmont and all the administrators will have a chance to get to know you. They'll see that you're more than the file they have on you, and they'll see it firsthand. This could be your ticket to freedom. It's great!" She planted a warm, happy kiss on my cheek.

"But," I began, "and this is a big but . . ."

"What did you say about my butt?" she quipped.

"But I don't even know if I can do this," I said. "I've never painted a mural."

"And Michelangelo never painted the ceiling of the Sistine Chapel before he did it," she countered.

"You've got more faith in me than I do," I told her.

"I didn't marry a one-trick pony," she said. "You're talented, Ray, and I want to see you explore your creativity. You'll see. You'll have fun."

Our conversation soon shifted to my exhibition in New York and the *Sports Illustrated* interview. I told her that it had gone extremely well, although I was a little worried that I might have been too candid.

"Get ready for the press, Ray," she warned me. "They're going to be pouring in on you, and they may not always see you as a success story. Writers and reporters can put whatever spin they want to on a story. Be honest and open, but don't give them more than they want."

Melanie's intuition was formidable, and her advice was invariably sound. She offered plenty of encouragement, admonishing me when she felt it was appropriate, and she provided direction without insisting that she set the course. The mutual freedom of expression in our relationship was something I'd never before experienced. Melanie made me feel good about myself. I hoped I did the same for her.

Over coffee in the morning, as her visit was about to end, Melanie was reading the previous day's *Hartford Courant* while I perused an art magazine she'd brought.

"Hey, here's something that would be worth tapping into!" she suddenly exclaimed.

"What's that?" I asked.

"It says here that Connecticut will be hosting the 1995 Special Olympics World Games," she pointed out. "Wouldn't it be cool if you could do something for them?"

I WASN'T ABLE TO begin work on the Fenway Park mural for a couple of months. Warden Belmont went on vacation, paints had to be ordered and shipped in, and I was putting in extra time with the theater group—preparing for a reading of original poetry by group members at the upcoming TIME program graduation ceremony. Accustomed to making works of art smaller than a standard driver's license, I was intimidated by the prospect of filling the eight-by-nine-foot space that Warden Belmont had chosen as the mural site. But as I began sketching the image on the wall, I began to feel good about the project. At the same time, as Melanie had predicted, I started having a succession of positive interactions with members of the administrative staff.

Shortly after I'd started applying paint to the wall, staff members began to stop and make small talk. Some of the first to warm up to me were the secretaries, who brought in extra doughnuts and, occasionally, an extra burger and fries for me. I listened as they talked among themselves about their families and swapped complaints about their jobs. After they began to invite me into such conversations, they would sometimes comment that I seemed more like a fellow staff member than an inmate. I thrived on such talk, of course, because it almost made me feel like a normal human being again.

A number of the guards also stopped by regularly to check on my progress and tell me baseball stories. It seemed that everyone had a Fenway Park story, whether it involved a favorite haunt where they drank beers after a game or a foul ball they'd nearly caught one afternoon. Warden Belmont told me about the first game he attended there, and he said he and his father felt like the park was their second home. When I painted the stadium advertisement boards, I carefully lettered the warden's name in the cardholder space in my rendering of a MasterCard. Even though he never mentioned it, I could tell that he took pride in this little detail.

The mural was a project that engaged people and invited conversation, speculation, open debate, and earnest sports banter. As Melanie had predicted, it made people feel good. Especially me.

When I reached the stage of the mural where the ballpark seats needed to be populated with spectators, I started getting special requests. Warden Belmont asked me to paint Joe DiMaggio and Ted Williams sitting together in the box seats behind home plate. One of the lieutenants showed me his favorite place to sit and asked me to paint a hot dog in one of his hands and a beer in the other. A secretary was rather coy after I obliged her request that I paint her into the picture sitting next to Elvis Presley. By the time I'd finished painting the lower forefront section of the stands, literally dozens of prison staff members were portrayed in the mural.

Sometimes the stories the mural evoked were of a highly personal nature. For example, one officer— a lively, robust man in his forties—approached me quietly one afternoon after I'd painted him into the scene.

"Ray," he commended me, "this is a fine piece of work, and I really appreciate being included in it." Then he added, "But I need to ask a favor of you."

"What's that, sir?" I inquired.

"Well, it looks like you painted a beer in my hand. Listen, I'm in the AA program, have been for going on thirteen years, and, well . . . maybe you could make that a cup of coffee instead?"

I happily turned the can into a cup.

Another officer—a big, older man who wore the stress of a career in corrections with a look of dull sadness—touched me deeply with a request he made after I'd already painted him into the scene. He told me that the mural was especially important to him because his son had been offered a tryout with the Red Sox. "He's been in the minors for almost ten years, and this is his big chance. He's a pitcher, Mattie," he told me. "Every time I look at this painting of yours, I imagine myself sitting in the stands and watching him play. It makes me feel real good to see this picture."

I thanked him for sharing his feelings with me, and I told him that I'd be praying for his son's success in making the team. But about two weeks later, looking very downcast, he approached me again.

"Danny didn't make the squad, Ray," he said sadly. "Says

he can't stay in the minors much longer, either, so he's going to be working the fishing boats."

"Jeez, I'm sorry, Mr. Everette," I said.

"I still really like your picture, though," he continued. "And I was wondering something." He pointed at a spot on the wall. "Maybe you could paint the number thirty-three on one of the pitchers' jerseys. That's been Danny's number ever since he was in high school. Then he'll always be a player, and I'll always be in the stands watching him."

I assured him that I'd be happy to change the number on one of the players' jerseys. Then, feeling his disappointment as acutely as if it were my own, tears formed in my eyes as I watched him walk away and considered that his dream for his child had been relegated to an image on a prison wall.

ONE MORNING WHEN I REPORTED to the front-office lobby to put the finishing touches on "the wall," as everyone referred to the mural, I found Warden Belmont standing in front of it with a small group of people, including the new deputy warden, Mr. Ford. They were debating the possible outcome of the game moment that I had depicted.

"Well, I don't care what you say, Kevin," Mr. Ford said to Warden Belmont. "You've got Don Mattingly at the plate, a man on first, and the Sox are only ahead by one run. Donny's due for a home run. He hits well under pressure."

Smiling broadly, Belmont turned to the group and explained, "He's a die-hard Yankees fan, folks. But I predict he's going to have his bubble burst." Then, noticing me, he said, "And speaking of die-hard Yankees fans, here's our resident artist, Ray Materson."

All eyes turned in my direction, and a woman who was fifty-ish and slightly stout, sporting a crop of windswept blond hair, stepped up to me and offered her hand.

"This is an absolutely marvelous painting," she said in a deep, raspy voice as she vigorously shook my hand. "Excellent job!"

"This is Mrs. Schmidt, Ray," Warden Belmont said. "She's the director of the Connecticut Special Olympics."

Sheila Schmidt, it turned out, had come to CRCI because Warden Belmont had contacted the Connecticut Special Olympics Committee to offer assistance in preparing for the World Games. With its free labor force, the prison was custom-made to help with civic ventures, and such arrangements were typically good for everyone involved. Inmates had an opportunity to become involved in a socially responsible endeavor, the project or agency in need received free help, and those in charge of the prison system got good publicity.

Sheila was so taken with the Fenway Park mural that she began brainstorming about how I might be commissioned to create one or more murals to celebrate the airlift that was being arranged to bring the handicapped Olympians from all over the country into Bradley International Airport in Windsor Locks, Connecticut. It would be months before a decision was reached on whether and how I might be involved in the program.

39. **Riot**

By the summer of 1994, I had been incarcerated for more than six years and would be eligible for parole in ten months. I had a good prison record; I'd paid off my back child support; I'd been involved in civic outreach, in the form of my antidrug poster; I'd contributed to the Connecticut Crime Victims fund; and I'd become something of a celebrity, interviewed by ABC-TV's *Good Morning America*, New York's WWOR-TV, and representatives from a variety of other local and national media outlets. In view of all this, I felt some confidence as I approached Warden Belmont to ask his permission that I be considered for weekend furloughs, which were allowed for inmates with good records. To my delight, he immediately set in motion the procedures necessary to make that happen.

Within two weeks' time I was moved off the main prison compound into Building Seven, an older, single- and double-room dormitory that originally had been used to house unmarried corrections officers. The approximately twenty inmates who occupied the building were all considered at low risk for attempting to escape or otherwise cause trouble and, for that reason, had been granted the privilege of leaving the compound on weekends. This was absolutely as good as it got in the prison system. My roommate was Ricky Tomasa, an excellent guitar player who had a singing voice that reminded me of Joe South's. I'd met him several months earlier in the chapel, where he regularly accompanied the prison choir as both singer and guitarist. Ricky was an old friend of Gino Calli's, and a recovering junkie, and I found him easy to get along with.

It was the end of June when Melanie came to pick me up at the prison for our first weekend together off the grounds. As we made the two-hour drive to her apartment in Albany, I could hardly believe that I was finally back out in the world. We stopped for burgers at a fast-food restaurant and went grocery shopping together, and I had the feeling that all eyes were on me. It was my dream come true, if only for a weekend: freedom!

The two-bedroom Main Street apartment that Melanie shared with John seemed palatial to me. We spent much of the day visiting yard sales and sitting on her porch talking, but it was the most exciting day I'd known in a very long time. That evening, after a meal of lasagna and Caesar salad, she said she had some important news.

"So," I asked, "what is it? Gallery news?"

With both caution and excitement in her voice, she said, "I'm pregnant, Ray."

The news caught me entirely off guard. I was as excited as I was anxious. We spent the rest of the night almost giddily trying out possible names for our child and discussing the future that, at last, seemed to be coming together for us. It was a happy time.

Three days later, less than three weeks after my transfer to Building Seven, as I sat on my bunk sewing an image based on a scene from *A Midsummer Night's Dream,* I thought about the life Melanie and I planned to share with each other, and I considered how richly I'd been blessed in virtually every aspect of my life. At that moment, I was infused with a feeling of goodness and warmth that matched the clear summer day outside.

"Yo, Ray," shouted Ricky, storming into the room, "I think something jumped off on the compound!"

Pulling off my headphones and climbing down from my bunk, I followed Ricky down the dorm's narrow corridor. Across from the C.O.'s office, we stepped through a door that led out into a small, fenced yard, where two C.O.s and several inmates already stood as they looked toward the main prison compound. Sirens wailed from that direction, and the radios attached to the guards' belts crackled and droned with commands:

"Moving to Building Two!"

"All officers, clear the yard!"

"Clear the circle! Clear the circle!"

As the increasingly frantic-sounding calls interrupted one another, the officers who were with us watched the scene in the distance with tense expressions that revealed their mixed feelings. They clearly had some desire to be with their comrades on the compound, but at the same time, they were understandably relieved to be safe with us, on the opposite side of the road.

A TV news van arrived, even before the state police and the Corrections Emergency Response Team showed up. A reporter brushed at his shirt and moved into the afternoon sunlight as a video operator set another camera in place to tape his report. Wild whoops, jeers, and the sounds of breaking glass could be heard in the background.

It took the riot squads several hours to bring the melee

under control. When the numbers were tallied, the report was tragic. A number of corrections officers had been injured, and at least three dozen inmates had been stabbed, beaten, or otherwise physically harmed. Two men who were serving only short sentences for nonviolent crimes had been brutally killed. One of them—a slight, soft-spoken black man—had been pulled from his bunk and stabbed through the heart as he prayed for his life. Another man had been chased down by a mob and, with the TV news cameras rolling, bludgeoned and knifed to death in the yard.

Seven or eight days later, I stood with Deputy Warden Ford in front of the Fenway Park mural. "This, Ray," he said, gesturing toward it, "is the opposite pole from what we saw last week. This is the part of corrections that I believe can promote healing and can make a difference."

"I believe that, too, sir," I agreed.

After a brief pause, I continued: "In the time that I've been incarcerated, I've seen some amazing, talented men—artists, writers, gifted people—behind bars. I wish the system would spend a little time helping those men, nuturing their talent and creativity. Because just as sure as people are born to create, I believe that if their talents and gifts aren't encouraged, they become destructive. Sometimes they destroy others, but more often, they destroy themselves."

Still looking at the painting, Warden Ford said, "What we need to do is offer that encouragement before the men land in prison, Ray. Got any ideas?"

"Yes, I do, sir," I responded. "Yes, I do."

40. TRANSFORMATION

Over the next several months I worked at my job as the official CRCI muralist—a job that put me at the top of the prison pay scale, making $1.75 a day. I painted murals in the prison post office, gymnasium, school, and chaplain's office. My subjects included basketball, stock-car racing, and architecture. Continuing to spend weekends with Melanie and John, I watched as the new child inside her grew. Melanie had been writing a screenplay, and—with earnings from my art sales combined with her own income—she was able to scrape together enough money to put a down payment on a little barn-shaped house on a lake just outside of Albany.

Meanwhile, I happily accepted a commission to create three embroidery images for the Special Olympics World Games. I worked feverishly on the pieces when I wasn't painting a mural, sewing new works to send to Aarne's gallery, or preparing for my scheduled January appearance before the state Board of Parole.

In October, the long-awaited article about me finally

appeared in *Sports Illustrated.* The two-page spread included photographs of my 1963 New York Yankees series as well as one of me posing alongside the Fenway Park mural. Warden Belmont was elated that the mural he'd commissioned had made it into his favorite magazine.

I had also been interviewed by the *New York Times,*

NBC-TV's *Today* show, and at least two local television news services. Melanie cautioned me to resist letting all the attention go to my head, but at the same time, I knew she was just as excited as I was.

When the day of my parole hearing finally arrived, I was transported to Somers prison along with three other inmates. We were all shackled together for the short trip, and when we arrived we were led into a large waiting area outside a conference room. As my wife, Melanie was allowed to meet me there and attend the hearing, but we weren't allowed to sit together. She was seven months pregnant by this time, and we smiled at each other from across the room.

Several other inmates were also seated in the waiting area. One by one, we were called before the board, and my stomach was knotted with tension as I waited my turn. Corrections officers stationed around the room glumly observed the men who were about to undergo a process with potentially life-changing consequences. My level of anxiety increased with each passing moment, even as Melanie kept smiling reassuringly at me. At last my name was called.

Still in leg shackles, I was led into the cold, dimly lit conference room. Two women and an elderly man were seated at a long table. I took a seat at a smaller table across from them.

"Materson," intoned one of the women, who wore glasses.

"That's me," I politely responded.

I had hoped the board members would want to talk about my artwork and all that had happened as a result of it. There was plenty of evidence that my life had been redeemed—the antidrug poster, my work in the TIME program, the favorable articles in the press, the many letters of recommendation—and they could see that I now had a lovely wife who was heavy with child. But they didn't seem to care. In a near monotone, the elderly man began reciting the charges to which I'd pleaded guilty. The woman wearing glasses then read snippets of the accompanying police reports. As I was reminded of all that I had done to justify being sent to prison, I felt intensely disheartened. Once again I was reduced to the status of thief and robber—a menace to society.

Then the other woman remarked, "I see here that you have received no disciplinary reports in your entire period of incarceration. That's quite good. You've avoided trouble."

"Avoiding trouble outside of prison is, of course, more difficult," said the man.

"You were very bad, Mr. Materson," said the woman wearing glasses.

The meeting was proceeding in a manner contrary to my hopes. I wanted to scream at the three people who held my life in their hands. "But look how I've changed my life!" I wanted to say to them. "Look at the good!"

That opportunity was granted when the gray-haired man said, "Tell us what you have done to better yourself while you've been incarcerated, Mr. Materson."

Softly, stammering a little, I began to talk. I told the board how I'd come to terms with my drug addiction and renewed my faith in God. Motioning slowly in Melanie's direction, I pointed out that I was now married and that my wife and I had a baby on the way.

After I finished speaking, I was excused from the room and told to wait for the board's decision. The entire hearing had taken little more than five minutes. Wondering how a decision could be made on the basis of such a brief interview, I had a bad feeling. I felt that, somehow, I had managed to blow it. Worst of all, I felt like a criminal—an entirely different matter from intellectually recognizing that one is a criminal. Another five minutes passed before I was called back into the conference room. I entered and sat down before the board.

"You have only served seven years of a twenty-five-year sentence," said the woman wearing glasses.

"Ten of that was suspended, of course," added the gray-haired man. "But you realize, Mr. Materson, that if you were to be released on parole, any violation could result in your being returned to prison to finish serving the entire twenty-five-year sentence. You do understand that, don't you?"

"Yes," I said, "I understand that."

"Then, although the board is split in its decision," he concluded, "we are awarding you conditional parole."

"You will be released on May second," said the woman in the glasses.

The knot in my belly loosened. "Thank you," I said, and I turned to see Melanie smiling broadly. The time had finally come for us to be together. Outside the conference room we hugged each other and cried.

DAVID HENRY MATERSON WAS BORN on March 24, 1995. Hugo M., who had become my AA sponsor, drove me to New York for an eight-day furlough after Melanie delivered the baby. I finished the Special Olympics commission by the end of April. The three pieces were photographed and reproduced as posters. Then, on May 2, Melanie picked me up from Carl Robinson Correctional Institute for the last time.

Art Index

Title page, *Opening Day*. 1997. Courtesy of Gary Alan Fine.
Page x, *The House on York Road*. 1994. Courtesy of William Louis-Dreyfus Collection.
Page 3, *Mickey Mantle*. 1996. Courtesy of William Louis-Dreyfus Collection.
Page 8, *Mea Maxima Culpa*. 1992. Courtesy of American Primitive Gallery.
Page 10, *Once a Young Man (Dad in Central Park)*. 1996. Courtesy of William Louis-Dreyfus Collection.
Page 12, *I Remember Papa*. 1991. Courtesy of Private Collection.
Page 17, *Still in Saigon*. 1989. Courtesy of Private Collection.
Page 21, *First Cigarette*. 1992. Courtesy of Collection of Sandi Blanda.
Page 24, *Anywhere Next Exit*. 1992. Courtesy of Private Collection.
Page 27, *Public School Girls*. 1994. Courtesy of Peter Brams Collection.
Page 32, *Bus Boy*. 1993. Courtesy of Private Collection.
Page 35, *Ogres All Stars (Sunday Afternoon)*. 1996. Courtesy of William Louis-Dreyfus Collection.
Page 37, *Impromptu Service*. 2001. Courtesy of American Primitive Gallery.
Page 39, *School Daze*. 1992. Courtesy of William Louis-Dreyfus Collection.
Page 40, *M.: Average White Girl*. 2002. Courtesy of Private Collection.
Page 43, *D.O.A. (The Last Rush)*. 1995. Courtesy of Private Collection.
Page 46, *The End*. 1992. Courtesy of Private Collection.
Page 48, *Kid with the Works*. 1993. Courtesy of Mr. And Mrs. V. J. Manieri.
Page 50, *Little Green Bags*. 1994. Courtesy of William Louis-Dreyfus Collection.
Page 52, *Till Death Do Us Part*. 1993. Courtesy of William Louis-Dreyfus Collection.
Page 54, *The Arrest*. 1991. Courtesy of Collection of Ed and Barbara-Rose Okun.
Page 58, *The Prisoner*. 1991. Courtesy of American Primitive Gallery.
Page 69, *Anywhere Next Exit*. 1994. Courtesy of Private Collection.
Page 73, *Shower Room*. 1998. Courtesy of Porter/Price Collection.
Page 74, *Demons and the Unseen Things*. 1994. Courtesy of Private Collection.
Page 77, *The Cup of His Blood (Hate Me)*. 1993. Courtesy of American Primitive Gallery.
Page 78, *The Seagull*. 1991. Courtesy of Private Collection.

Page 83, *Vision of Paradise*. 1996. Courtesy of Private Collection.
Page 85, *Bo (Give 'Em Hell Bo!)*. 1998. Courtesy of Private Collection.
Page 99, *Titania and Oberon*. 1996. Courtesy of Private Collection.
Page 102, *My Fate Cries Out*. 1989. Courtesy of Private Collection.
Page 107, *Girl in Mirror*. 1991. Courtesy of William Louis-Dreyfus Collection.
Page 110, *Broken Trust*. 1992. Courtesy of Collection of the Artist.
Page 112, *Rock and Roll Girl*. 1992. Courtesy of Collection of Melanie Materson.
Page 121, *Major Mom*. 1991. Courtesy of American Primitive Gallery.
Page 122, *Conscientious Objector*. 1995. Courtesy of Private Collection.
Page 125, *Boot Story*. 1995. Courtesy of Private Collection.
Page 135, *Gino: Life x 6, The Noon Watch J2*. 1997. Courtesy of William Louis-Dreyfus Collection.
Page 138, *The Pursuit of Happiness*. 1997. Courtesy of American Primitive Gallery.
Page 142, *Don't Get Pulled In*. 1992. Courtesy of Peter Brams Collection.
Page 148, *Involuntary Blue*. 1995. Courtesy of Private Collection.
Page 149, *Lake Michigan*. 1991. Courtesy of Collection of Melanie Materson.
Page 154, *Unheavenly Host*. 1995. Courtesy of Private Collection.
Page 163, *Waiting for the Man*. 1997. Courtesy of William Louis-Dreyfus Collection.
Page 170, *Lady with a Plan*. 1997. Courtesy of William Louis-Dreyfus Collection.
Page 175, *Whitey Ford*. 1993. Courtesy of William Louis-Dreyfus Collection.
Page 175, *Roger Maris*. 1993. Courtesy of William Louis-Dreyfus Collection.
Page 175, *Shoeless Joe Jackson*. 1995. Courtesy of Private Collection.
Page 175, *Elston Howard*. 1993. Courtesy of William Louis-Dreyfus Collection.
Page 182, *The Trailer Visit*. 1994. Courtesy of William Louis-Dreyfus Collection.
Page 186, *CRCI Softball Champs Bldg 6*. 1995. Courtesy of William Louis-Dreyfus Collection.
Page 200, *Self-Portrait: The Fenway Mural*. 1995. Courtesy of Private Collection.
Page 202, *Special Olympics: World Games*. 1995. Courtesy of World Games. Special Olympics in memory of Shela Schmidt.
Page 203, *The Guitar Man*. 1995. Courtesy of Private Collection.
Page 206, *Failure to Appear*. 1995. Courtesy of Victoria Wilson.
Page 208, *The Screenwriter*. 1995. Courtesy of William Louis-Dreyfus Collection.
Page 210, *The Parole Board*. 1995. Courtesy of American Primitive Gallery.
Page 212, *Metamorphosis*. 1997. Courtesy of Private Collection.